Quotes from reviewers

"If having a loving, open, honest relationship is your first priority, this book is a must-read! Every couple who takes the time to make their own Couples Contract will enhance their relationship now and in the future."

> Mary Dee Dickerson, PhD, CFP, author of *Grow Your Goals*

"This book belongs on the bookshelf of every couple as well as lawyers, psychologists, counselors, and financial professionals. The Couples Contract is a landmark concept that will nurture, encourage and enhance mature and loving relationships. Attorneys Sherman and Janke brilliantly pull off a difficult balancing act, showing sensitivity to emotional and relationship concerns while thoroughly addressing legal issues."

> Jonathan Rich, PhD, author of *The Couple's Guide to Love & Money*

"Unlike so many books that help couples divorce, this book provides a refreshing idea for enhancing the relationship and affirming the couple's commitment. I will be referring my clients to this book."

> Maureen C. Kenny, PhD, Psychologist, co-chair Publications Committee, American Counseling Association

"This book is an invaluable resource, a must read for all couples."

> David Olsen, PhD, co-author of *The Couples Survival Workbook*

"As .... ho for 30 y .... more love .... we had reservations about a contract for couples. Then we read the book and understood that this is not a traditional legal contract about power and control, but a tool that will cultivate, preserve and protect the highest love between two persons. We highly recommend this book!"

> Barry Vissell, MD and Joyce Vissell, RN, MS, authors of *The Shared Heart*, *The Heart's Wisdom*, and *Meant To Be*

"With the Couples Contract, it is possible to create a document that can help safeguard your mutual affection. This unique and valuable resource honors your love and trust, and is determined to help you keep it that way."

> Peter Pearson, PhD, co-founder of The Couples Institute, Menlo Park, CA

"I can't think of a better booster for a happy, healthy, lasting relationship."

> Gary W. Silverman, CFP, host of Money$Talk, financial commentator for KFDX and KAUZ

"Sherman and Janke write in a clear, concise fashion that allows the reader easy access to a relationship contract that is loving, pro-marriage, and beneficial. I will suggest the Couples Contract to all of my couples. Read it, love it, but most importantly, use it!"

> Rev. Russell K. Elleven, EdD, LPC, CFLE

"I am giving this book to every client in a committed relationship. A Couples Contract is the foundation for a lasting, loving arrangement and assures that future disagreements are minimized."

> Bert Whitehead, MBA, JD, financial advisor, author of *Facing Financial Dysfunction: Why Smart People Do Stupid Things with Money*

"This book reveals a void that exists between legal books and relationship counseling books, and then fills it. I would like to see this book in the hands of every couple. It will prevent many breakups, divorces, and children growing up in one-parent families."

> Sylvia Weishaus, PhD, Sherman Oaks, co-founder of Making Marriage Work

"*The Couples Contract for a Lasting Relationship* should be required reading for all couples."

> Mary Heléne Rosenbaum, executive director of the Dovetail Institute for Interfaith Family Resources

"The Couples Contract will become a standard part of my practice. It is an ideal approach for couples who are serious about making a lasting commitment."

> Dawn Elaine Bowie, JD, family law attorney

"I have already referred one young couple to the book and look forward to having it as a resource for my clients and friends."

> Sharon Rich, EdD, financial planner, founder of PridePlanners

"The Couples Contract is an exciting tool that I use in my practice. I like that it is first about caring for each other and keeping the relationship together while it goes about addressing financial issues and creating a framework for making decisions. The Couples Countract helps make stronger relationships."

> Dana J. Levit, CFP, president of PridePlanners

"Counselors, attorneys, mediators and their clients can benefit from *The Couples Contract for a Lasting Relationship*. This book offers a plan for working through issues that tear people apart. Kudos to Sherman and Janke."

> Prof. Duane Ruth-Heffelbower, MDiv, JD, Fresno Pacific University

"*The Couples Contract for a Lasting Relationship* is filled with valuable insights and practical tools for couples."

> Georgia Shaffer, Psychologist, Life Coach, speaker, author

"I can't imagine anyone in a serious relationship who wouldn't have a need for your book."

> J. Steven Cowen, CFP, Steven Cowen & Associates

"Every couple should read this book. The Couples Contract provides you with easy to follow steps on how to write a contract with heart—a contract that honors the 'we' in your relationship while respecting and protecting the 'I' of each of you." Great material. Well done.

> Dr. Mackenzie Brooks, PhD, couples counselor, trainer, Victoria, BC

"The Couples Contract is a creative resource and wake-up call to all couples to be proactive in defining the terms of their union. No therapist should be without a copy of this resource. In fact, I will keep extra copies to give to my clients."

> Ellyn Bader, PhD, cofounder of The Couples Institute

"I think this book is excellent. It is clear and easy to use as a reference...a great resource for couples. The list of questions in Chapter 4 is very useful—it will help people make informed decisions."

> Robin Seigle, National Conflict Resolution Center

"Financial issues cause more than 50% of all relationship failures. That's why this book is a must-read for couples, therapists and financial advisors. The wisdom in these pages will save relationships."

> William C. Cuthbertson, MBA, CFP, The Fiscalis Group

"*The Couples Contract for a Lasting Relationship* can save couples and their children endless heartache and enormous amounts of money. It would be a better world if all lawyers approached marriage the way Sherman and Janke do."

> John W. Jacobs, MD, couples therapist, author of *All You Need Is Love and Other Lies About Marriage*

"As a family lawyer who works with couples to build premarital and postmarital agreements, I use the Couples Contract to show clients the potential benefits of these agreements. I have adapted many provisions from this book for agreements that I draft for clients."

> Forrest S. Mosten, Certified Family Law Specialist, author of *Complete Guide to Mediation and Unbundling Legal Services*

"*The Couples Contract for a Lasting Relationship* is essential for any committed couple. It guides them through some of the most important decisions they will ever make and, in the process, they will gain a better understanding of their core values and deepen their relationship. I will make sure every couple I work with reads this book."

> Nancy J. Ross, LCSW, Therapist, Mediator, Co-founder of Collaborative Divorce

"A valuable reference for anyone in a committed relationship and professional advisors. The Couples Contract's unique twist is using a contract to improve the quality of relationships, in addition to providing a thorough discussion of financial issues and legal rights of partners."

> Prof. Barbara O'Neill, PhD, CFP, CRPC, AFC, CHC, CFCS, Financial Resource Management, Rutgers

www.nolocouples.com

❝ What are the most useful and constructive things a loving couple can accomplish with a written agreement? **❞**

Ask a better question, define a better goal, and you get a better result. This fully explains why the Couples Contract is so different from—and superior to—traditional contracts prepared by traditional attorneys. It produces a document that is so useful and important that every couple in a committed relationship should have one.

❝ If you are like most couples, when you hear the word "contract" in the context of your relationship, you probably wrinkle your nose and turn away. This is because, until now, you've never seen or heard of a contract for couples that is loving, useful and constructive. **❞**

WITHDRAWN

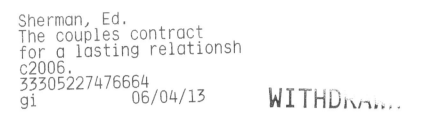

The Couples Contract
for a
Lasting Relationship

For all couples ~ married, getting married, unmarried

by Attorneys Ed Sherman and Bruce Janke

Nolo Press
o c c i d e n t a l
501 Mission Street, Suite 2
Santa Cruz, CA 95060
(831) 466-9922

THIS BOOK WAS PRINTED IN
JANUARY 2006

FREE UPDATE NOTICES
We review laws of 50 states each January
and whenever we reprint. Look for news
and changes at www.nolocouples.com

© 2006 by Charles E. Sherman

ISBN: 0-944508-58-8   ISBN13/EAN: 978-0944-50858-9

Library of Congress Control Number: 2005932883

Design and graphics:	Ed Sherman
Art:	Linda Allison
Cover design:	Ed Sherman
Cover photo:	Richard May

About the authors

Ed Sherman, a family law attorney since 1970, founded Nolo Press with *How to Do Your Own Divorce in California*. Through his several books on divorce and relationships, creation of the independent paralegal movement, and his co-founding of Divorce Helpline and Couples Helpline, he has made it his life's work to keep family problems out of the adversarial court system by making the legal process understandable, affordable and accessible for all.

Bruce Janke, California attorney, has practiced civil litigation in state and federal trial and appellate courts since 1977, including three years devoted exclusively to consumer protection and 15 years in family law and adoptions. He is a former instructor at Santa Clara University Institute for Paralegal Education and at the American College of Switzerland.

Acknowledgments

We are indebted to many outstanding professionals who contributed important insights and suggestions. It is impossible to rank them, so they appear here alphabetically. Our heartfelt thanks and gratitude go to:

Dawn Elaine Bowie, JD, family law attorney

William C. Cuthbertson, MBA, CFP, The Fiscalis Group

Rev. Russell K. Elleven, EdD, LPC, CFLE

John W. Jacobs, MD, couples therapist,
   author of *All You Need is Love and Other Lies About Marriage*

Maureen C. Kenny, PhD, co-chair Publications Committee, American
   Counseling Association

Dana J. Levit, CFP, financial planner, president of PridePlanners

Prof. Barbara O'Neill, PhD, CFP, CRPC, AFC, CHC, CFCS,
   Financial Resource Management, Rutgers

Jonathan Rich, PhD, author of *The Couple's Guide to Love & Money*

Sharon Rich, EdD, financial planner, founder of PridePlanners

Mary Heléne Rosenbaum, executive director of the Dovetail Institute for Interfaith Family Resources and editor of *Dovetail: A Journal by and for Jewish/Christian Families*.

Nancy J. Ross, LCSW, therapist, mediator, cofounder of Collaborative Divorce

Robin Seigle, National Mediation Center

Gary W. Silverman, CFP, financial and investment advisor, host of Money$Talk, commentator for KFDX and KAUZ

Sylvia Weishaus, PhD, Sherman Oaks, co-founder of Making Marriage Work

Bert Whitehead, MBA, JD, financial advisor, author of *Facing Financial Dysfunction: Why Smart People Do Stupid Things with Money*

and

Nolo staffers Joe Cosentino and Sandra Borland

Table of Contents

Part One ~ The basic Couples Contract

Part Two ~ Beyond the basic

Part Three ~ Completing your agreement

How a written agreement can benefit your relationship

> **❝** What are the most useful and constructive things a loving couple can accomplish with a written agreement? **❞**

Ask a better question, define a better goal, and you get a better result. This fully explains why the Couples Contract is so different from—and superior to—traditional contracts prepared by traditional attorneys. It produces a document that is so useful and important that every couple in a committed relationship should have one.

This book introduces a new approach to agreements made by committed couples that is entirely different from traditional contracts such as premarital, marital and living-together agreements. The features of such contracts can be incorporated, but they are not the point of what we are doing here. By redefining the purpose of the contract, we achieve a relationship agreement with positive and constructive features so valuable that no couple should be without one, and a document so different from traditional contracts drafted by traditional attorneys that it deserves a new name to distinguish it, so we call it the **Couples Contract**.

A. Pit Bulls and Golden Retrievers

If you are like most couples, when you hear the word "contract" in the context of your relationship, you probably wrinkle your nose and turn away. This is because, until now, you've never seen or heard of a contract for couples that is loving, useful and constructive. It's as if you had grown up on an island where the only dogs were edgy Pit Bulls, so when someone says "dog," you can't imagine anything else because you've never seen or heard of dogs like Golden Retrievers that love kids and can lead the blind.

In this sense, a traditional contract is like a Pit Bull that makes people uncomfortable to be around, and the Couples Contract is like a Golden Retriever: they are both dogs, but, oh, so different! You are like a person who has never seen or heard of a friendly, useful dog, and we are a Golden Retriever sales team. We know how wonderful our pooch really is, how much it can help you and improve your life, and we know you will want one if you just take a look and give it a chance.

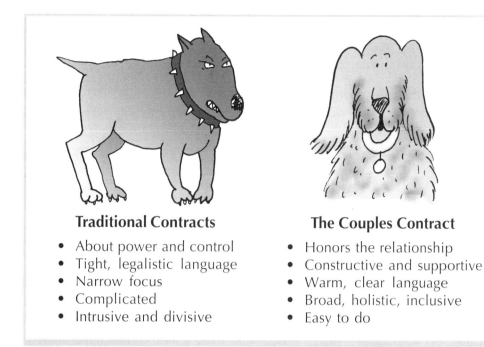

Traditional Contracts

- About power and control
- Tight, legalistic language
- Narrow focus
- Complicated
- Intrusive and divisive

The Couples Contract

- Honors the relationship
- Constructive and supportive
- Warm, clear language
- Broad, holistic, inclusive
- Easy to do

The trouble with traditional contracts

Traditional contracts, which couples justifiably regard like a root-canal, arouse concern and put people off for two basic reasons (among many):

- They are entirely about power and control—defining who owns income and assets, and who gets what when there is a death or breakup; and,
- Traditional attorneys and their contracts, written in sphincter-tightening legalese, fail to honor and reflect the couple's love, trust and affection.

Premarital agreements in particular have so often been nasty, money-grubbing things, used to strip a woman of rights when she marries a wealthy man, that many states have imposed strict limitations, trying to make sure she really knows what she's giving up and that her agreement is not *unconscionably* unfair. (Apparently, a certain degree of unfairness is acceptable.)

This is why couples believe that going to lawyers to get a contract will intrude on their relationship and undermine the things they hold most dear.

There's a better way!

Contracts have a long, honorable history, but have not been put to good use for modern couples simply because no one thought to do it—until now. In this book, we have morphed traditional contracts for married and unmarried couples into a new relationship agreement, the Couples Contract. It is a different animal entirely—affirming and forward-looking—whose whole purpose is to do constructive things for loving couples.

Seeking to do the most good

The Couples Contract seeks to use the tools of law to do the most good for the couple and to add features to their relationship that can only help. From this premise, everything flows that makes the Couples Contract a good thing.

Honor the relationship. To do good for the couple, the contract and the process that produces it must honor and support the loving relationship.

Positive, clear language. We avoid the impenetrable language that lawyers tend to use, often as an awkward substitute for clear thinking and competent writing. The Couples Contract is written as much as possible in loving and affirming language and at all times in simple terms that everyone can understand.

Constructive features. Where a traditional contract seeks to define and control income and assets, usually to benefit one party over the other, the Couples Contract seeks ways to benefit the couple and their relationship, so the subject matter tends to be different from the traditional contracts, as you will see below.

B. What you can accomplish with a Couples Contract

The advantages of the Couples Contract can be had by any couple at any time. It doesn't matter if you are married, soon-to-be married, or simply living together. If you are a committed couple, you should have at least a basic Couples Contract. In fact, you can't afford to be without one. Here's why:

The basic Couples Contract

In the basic agreement, you get very important advantages without having to go into discussions of finances or other details of your relationship. Just fill in the blanks and you get these essential benefits:

- Make a loving commitment to a lasting relationship
- Make clear that you have a high degree of openness, honesty and good faith in all dealings with one another
- Build successful problem-solving into your relationship
- Keep the terms of your relationship stable, no matter where you move

- Put a safety net under your relationship by making sure your relationship never ends up in court
- Reduce the fear of commitment and/or marriage by creating safety

Very easy to do. Your basic agreement does not alter any rights or duties under the laws of your home state in any way other than to choose mediation and arbitration as your preferred method to solve problems, should the need arise. This is why anyone can do it without legal advice or assistance. How to do your own basic Couples Contract is described in chapter 2.

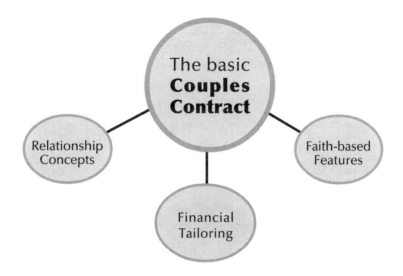

Beyond the basics

You don't have to, but if you want, you can add some features to your basic agreement that *will* take some thought and discussion, such as:

- Adjusting (tailoring) your financial relationships to make them more suitable to your needs. For some couples this will be very useful (chapter 5), while for unmarried couples the need is absolute and urgent (chapter 7).
- Introducing faith-related principles into your family life (chapter 6)

You can start with the simple basic agreement first, then tailor it later or never, or you can tailor your agreement at the outset. In either case, your agreement can be modified at any time by following the steps described in chapter 9G.

* * *

Now, let's take a closer look at the basic features.

Basic features

1. Make commitments

The Couples Contract opens with your commitment to a lasting relationship based upon mutual affection, respect and friendship. This sets the tone for the rest of your loving, constructive agreement.

Next, you commit yourselves to a high degree of openness, honesty and good faith when dealing with one another. Writing down your commitment to what the law calls the "fiduciary duty"—discussed in chapter 2B(2)—creates a positive tone for your agreement and a strong foundation for your relationship.

Married. In some states, married couples owe a fiduciary duty to one another as a matter of law, but in most states it is either not made clear or, as in three states, specifically made an issue of fact to be proved in court. So, it is far better for you to affirmatively commit to this high standard in your Couples Contract.

Unmarried[1]. Unmarried couples are treated as strangers who do not have a high duty when dealing with one another unless it can be proved in court that a higher standard must be imposed because of the circumstances of the relationship.

Every couple should make this high standard of care a clearly stated principle of their relationship; that way there's no doubt about it in any state you live in now or might some day move to. It sounds good, feels good, and is a good thing to do.

---

[1] **Same-sex couples.** In the context of the Couples Contract, legal issues facing unmarried couples are mostly the same, no matter what their sexual orientation. In 3 or 4 states where same-sex unions are recognized, couples who register a Civil Union or Domestic Partnership gain rights almost equivalent to marriage and all discussions in this book addressed to married couples apply equally to them, except for one problem: the likelihood that a sister state will not recognize their relationship if it does not already exist there.

2. Build successful problem-solving into your relationship

One of the most important features you can add to any relationship—a gift that you can give yourselves—is planning in advance, while things are smooth and lovely, what you will do if your relationship wanes in the future. If you want a lasting relationship, there are specific things you can do to increase your chances.

The purpose of this section in the Couples Contract is to plant some seeds (or lay a foundation) that will help you unravel predicaments that come up for most couples sooner or later. Most couples have no plan or idea for how to deal with downturns in their relationship if they ever do occur, but not you—your Couples Contract is there to remind you that you won't sit idle because there are things you can do and resources you can turn to. You needn't do anything now (although reading a bit about it wouldn't hurt), because just having these ideas in the back of your mind will help you recognize signs that your relationship needs some attention, and you'll have some ideas for how to respond if that happens. Look at this as a form of free health insurance for your relationship.

What keeps couples together

Your Couples Contract states (and reminds you) that your intention is to preserve your mutual affection, respect and friendship, because this is the first principle of a lasting relationship. We didn't make it up: this is the conclusion of Dr. John Gottman, a towering figure in couples counseling, who achieved this insight after more than thirty years of research. In his bestselling book, *The Seven Principles for Making Marriage Work*, he discusses what keeps couples together and finds, among other things, that relationship problems can be resolved better by working first to reinforce your mutual positive feelings because "friendship fuels the flames of romance."

> ". . . happy marriages are based on a deep friendship. By this I mean a mutual respect for and enjoyment of each other's company. [Such] couples tend to know each other intimately.... They have an abiding regard for each other and express this fondness not just in the big ways, but in little ways day in and day out."[2]

However intense or frequent their battles, the couples that last have never lost their fondness and respect for one another. After describing the kinds of behavior that undermine mutual regard, Gottman describes seven things that happy marriages have in common, then shows how to introduce those seven principles

[2] John Gottman, *The Seven Principles for Making Marriage Work*. Three Rivers Press (2000), page 19.

into your own relationship. So, if ever you feel the ties that bind are weakening, this book would be a good place to start looking for things you can do about it. If you would rather look at a video or listen to a tape, the material is also available in audio or video form at www.gottman.com, where you can also learn about workshops conducted by The Gottman Institute. Other good books and resources are listed in Appendix C.

Additional factors that contribute to relationship success include learning to express your feelings, both positive and negative; learning to disagree in ways that are not destructive; and learning to accept things you can't change.

Beyond self-help

Beyond information in books, tapes and videos, there are couples workshops. Some might find it more effective to go directly to a good couples counselor. If one of you is allergic to the idea of counseling or therapy, look for a couples *coach*, which might be more acceptable. Enter "couples coach" into Google and see what comes up, or ask a recommended therapist to serve as a coach. Many religious organizations have trained conciliators who work with couples and many clergy are trained in couples counseling. In any case, you should only work with someone who is trained, experienced and certified to do the job. The important thing is that you not sit on your hands if one of you begins to feel that your mutual regard is fading. If you are committed to your relationship, you need to make it a priority, meaning there will be times when you have to put extra effort into it—get information, go to a workshop, get help. Above all, try to discuss things you can do to increase mutual regard and affection and decide together what steps to take.

Relationship Resources

Our companion CD has a fine article, *How to Get the Most From Couples Therapy*. Appendix C lists relationship resources that professionals have told us they recommend to their own clients. One we like is *The Five Love Languages*, by Dr. Gary Chapman who points out that people have different ways of expressing and receiving love, so that one person might be expressing it in a way that the other does not get, as where a man works hard to earn material things for his loved one and buys her gifts, but she craves touching and nice words. It's a matter of getting your signals straight.

Other resources include the highly regarded Couple Communication workshops, which have to date trained over 600,000 people and are conducted across the U.S. by thousands of certified instructors. To find an instructor near you, visit www.couplecommunication.com.

Then there's the respected Marriage Encounter with nationwide programs for troubled couples that are "based on Judeo-Christian concepts," though you need not be religious or belong to a religious organization in order to participate. You can find more information about them at www.marriage-encounter.org.

But wait! There's more! There's a mountain of good books, tapes, videos and workshops out there that you can substitute for our examples. Go out and browse or ask your clergy, counselors or other resource people. Time spent on this subject will be richly rewarded. That's the whole point—to make the effort.

3. Avoid surprises if you move

The rules that govern your relationship are determined primarily by the laws of the state you live in and these rules can change drastically when you move from one state to another. However, your Couples Contract helps you avoid surprises by declaring that the laws of your home state (where you reside when you make your agreement) will always govern your relationship, no matter where you live. If you move and find you like some rules in your new state better, you can modify your agreement (chapter 9G). Be sure to have your agreement reviewed by a family law attorney in your new state just before or right after you actually move there (see chapter 3B).

4. Put a safety net under your relationship

This section of your Couples Contract by itself makes it worth doing, because it gets you a huge advantage for no cost and little effort. The safety net—which should be a feature of every relationship—will make it very unlikely that your family problems will ever end up in court. Instead, if you ever stand on the brink of a breakup and face problems you can't resolve on your own or with counseling, you agree to use mediation and binding arbitration, which is a thousand times better than going to court for settling family matters.

In a survey of couples, when asked what percentage of all couples break up, most people answered correctly: about 50%. But when asked what they thought the chance was that *they* might ever break up, the *median*[3] answer was *zero!* No happy couple thinks they will ever break up, yet about half eventually do. The figure is more than 50% where one person is on a second or third marriage, and very much higher for unmarried couples. If you have no prearranged plan to avoid court, then if things ever go wrong, chances are that one of you will go to an attorney and the attorney will take the case into court, which is what they do. Far better if you agree ahead of time not to go there, ever.

Like free insurance

When you buy disability insurance, you don't intend to become disabled, but if the price is right, you'll get the insurance "just in case." It's exactly the same here, except it's completely free! You don't intend or expect to ever break up—and you've already planted seeds for problem-solving to help make sure you don't— but if it ever *were* to happen, what would you do? Without this part of your agreement, if faced with a situation that can't be resolved, you'd have no guidance and no alternative other than to give up or get a lawyer and go to court. Neither is acceptable; both are more likely to cause problems than to solve them.

The adversarial legal system is the worst possible place to take a family dispute, a forum where it is almost certain to get stirred up into something ugly and expensive. But now you can make sure your relationship and family matters are unlikely to ever end up in court. Instead, your Couples Contract says that if anything comes up that you can't resolve, you will go to mediation first (which has a high success rate), and if that doesn't solve it, you'll take the problem to binding and final arbitration. Believe us when we tell you that, based upon our combined experience with thousands of cases, this is far better than the alternative. You want this clause!

Mediation and arbitration are often referred to together as *alternative dispute resolution* (ADR), which has long been known to have many advantages over going to court. Court hearings and records are open to the public, while ADR is private and discreet. More important, courts are slow, complicated, expensive, and impersonal. If you were ever to end up there, the judge won't know you or your family and won't have much time or patience to learn about you or your problems. In our careers, we have almost never heard of a judge doing anything to try to save a relationship. By contrast, when you select your mediator, you can

---

[3] *Median = the value at the exact middle of all replies when arranged in numerical order.*

pick someone with a talent for conciliation who can take some time to explore solutions for your problems, including possible reconciliation.

A mediator tries to help parties work toward a solution to their dispute, but arbitration, like court, is also an adversarial proceeding where parties present facts and a decision is imposed. However, it is much more informal than court and conducted in a conference room by a paid arbitrator or a three-arbitrator panel instead of a judge. Arbitrators hear evidence and make a binding decision that can be filed with the court and enforced as a judgment. If you decide to use a three-arbitrator panel, one method is to have each party select one arbitrator and to have those two select a third. Two of the arbitrators can be anyone you choose, perhaps someone who knows your family and your values.

Another plus for ADR is that mediators and arbitrators can give attention to parts of your agreement that a court would not. A mediator might help you settle lifestyle conflicts, like housework or money handling, which a judge would not touch. If a couple agreed to raise their children according to a certain religious faith, a judge would probably ignore that provision because the Constitution requires separation of church and state; but arbitrators don't work for the state so they can include religious or lifestyle portions of your agreement in their decision.

5. Reduce fear of commitment and marriage

Because he sees it so often in his practice, Manhattan psychiatrist and professor John W. Jacobs, MD,[4] thinks many people are afraid of commitment and marriage because they fear the terrible emotional and financial costs of breakup. He believes that clear agreements in the Couples Contract about how the couple will handle decision-making, finances, and resolution of conflicts, will allow couples to feel safer about committing or getting married.

C. Beyond the basics

As you will learn in chapters 3–7, there are features that can be added to the basic contract—and for some couples, some things that *should* be added—but, unless you have a pressing need, you don't have to do it immediately.

- You can do a basic Couples Contract now and modify it later (chapter 9G) to add financial or other features that take more time to discuss and work out. This puts your agreement in place, gets you many important

---

[4] Author of *All You Need Is Love and Other Lies About Marriage*

advantages right away, and gives you time to work out the financial or other matters when it's convenient and comfortable.

- If you keep the basic Couples Contract basic and don't add more terms to it, your financial and parenting affairs will be governed by the laws of the state in which you live when you sign your contract. Chapter 5 discusses how financial tailoring works, how to learn about the laws of your state, and how to find out if tailoring might be to your advantage.

D. So easy, you can do it yourself

Doing the basic Couples Contract is sooooo, easy! Anyone can do it; all you need to do is check some boxes and fill in some blanks. Instructions and tips for doing your own basic Couples Contract are found in chapter 2A.

E. Example of a Basic Couples Contract

So you can see what a completed basic agreement looks like, here is an example Couples Contract for a couple who are soon to be married. With only a few minor changes—described in chapter 2—it will also work for a married or unmarried couple. As you can see, it is only five pages long, plus a signature page. The Couples Contract is printed here in the Poetica Chancery font. The files on the CD use a standard font likely to be found on most computers, but if you use the word processor method to do your contract, you can use any font you like (so long as it is easy to read) to get a look that pleases you. We suggest you print your agreement on high-quality paper or parchment—something suitable to the importance of this document in your lives.

Relationship Affirmations and Agreement
of Chris Brown and Jamie Jones

In loving anticipation of a lasting relationship, this agreement is made between Chris Brown and Jamie Jones, called by our first names in this agreement.

1. **Purpose.** *The purpose of our agreement is:*

    A.   To affirm our commitment to one another and to a lasting relationship based upon trust, mutual respect, affection and friendship.

    B.   To establish principles that will help us resolve personal issues that might threaten to weaken our relationship, should any ever arise.

    C.   To entirely and forever remove our relationship from the adversarial court system by committing to resolve disagreements of any nature that might arise between us, that we cannot resolve privately, by mediation or arbitration.

    D.   To govern our relationship rights and obligations according to the laws of Texas, except as modified by this agreement.

    E.   To create stability and predictability by governing our relationship rights and obligations according to the terms of this agreement no matter where we might reside in the future.

2. **Commitments**

In the making of this agreement and forever after, we affirm our close and confidential relationship and commit ourselves to mutual respect, openness, honesty, and the highest standards of good faith and fair dealing with one another in all matters, putting each other's best interests equal to our own.

3. **Effective date and duration of agreement**

Our agreement will become effective when we marry. If we do not marry, it will be of no effect. Once it takes effect, our agreement will remain in effect indefinitely, or until we sign a written agreement to modify or revoke it.

4. Principles for a lasting relationship

We believe that a lasting relationship is based upon trust, mutual respect, affection and friendship. It is our goal to preserve and reinforce these features in our union.

We believe that a lasting relationship sometimes requires an intentional effort, that reinforcing positive features is essential, and that practices learned from couples counseling have an excellent record of success.

If ever circumstances arise that threaten to undermine our mutual regard, we agree to make an effort to reinforce positive qualities in our relationship and resolve issues that weaken them.

We agree that if one of us requests it, we will set aside some quiet time to discuss our relationship together and seek ways to reinforce the positive features that are vital to our well-being as a couple. We will look for information in books, tapes or videos, starting with Dr. John Gottman's material on The Seven Principles for Making Marriages Work, and we will look at Dr. Gary Chapman's material about The Five Love Languages. We will also consider going to conciliation, or to a couples workshop, or to a couples coach or counselor.

5. Parenting

We agree that, except as modified by this agreement, our rights and duties as parents of any children born to or legally adopted by us will be governed by Texas law.

6. Money, property and financial matters

Except as modified by this agreement, we agree that all of our mutual rights and obligations with respect to our financial affairs, including our income, debts, and property, will be governed by Texas law no matter where we might live in the future.

7. Disclosures

Our agreement does not alter financial rights and duties under Texas law, therefore:

I, Chris, am sufficiently aware of Jamie's financial circumstances and freely and voluntarily give up the right to formal written disclosure or any other information about Jamie's finances.

I, Jamie, am sufficiently aware of Chris's financial circumstances and I freely and voluntarily give up the right to formal written disclosure or any other information about Chris's finances.

8. Representation and drafting

Chris and Jamie drafted this agreement together, jointly.

I, Chris, understand that I have the right to be represented by an independent attorney in the negotiation and preparation of this agreement and I have sufficient funds to retain an attorney for this purpose if I want one. Nonetheless, I choose not to be represented. I understand the terms of this agreement and have had ample opportunity to seek the advice an attorney or any other kind of advisor. I have read this agreement carefully and have received as much advice as I wish to receive. I freely and voluntarily choose to sign it without being represented by an attorney at this time.

I, Jamie, understand that I have the right to be represented by an independent attorney in the negotiation and preparation of this agreement and I have sufficient funds to retain an attorney for this purpose if I want one. Nonetheless, I choose not to be represented. I understand the terms of this agreement and have had ample opportunity to seek the advice of an attorney or any other kind of advisor. I have read this agreement carefully and have received as much advice as I wish to receive. I freely and voluntarily choose to sign it without being represented by an attorney at this time.

9. Resolution of disputes—mediation and arbitration

It is our desire to remove our relationship entirely and forever from the adversarial court system and to resolve any dispute that might arise between us or under this agreement by mediation and arbitration.

A. Mediation

1. *If we are unable to resolve any dispute ourselves or with counseling, then we each agree to make a reasonable good-faith effort to resolve the matter in mediation. On the written request of either party we will within thirty days submit our dispute to mediation with a mediator agreed upon by both of us. Unless we agree otherwise, our mediator must be a family law attorney who specializes in family law mediation in Texas. If we are unable to agree on a mediator, we will each choose one person to make a choice on our behalf, and those two persons together will appoint our mediator. We will participate in mediation in good faith and pay the cost of mediation from marital funds, if available, and if marital funds are not available, we will each be responsible for half the cost of such mediation.*

2. *We are each entitled to representation in mediation by an attorney of our choice. Attorney fees will be paid from marital funds, if available, and if marital funds are not available, each party will be responsible for his or her own attorney's fees.*

B. Arbitration

1. In the event that mediation does not resolve all issues within a reasonable number of sessions, then on the written request of either of us, <u>WE WILL SUBMIT THE MATTER TO BINDING ARBITRATION</u> within ninety days. The arbitrator will be agreed upon by both of us, but must be a family law professional in Texas: either an attorney who specializes in mediation or arbitration, or a retired family court judge. If we are unable to agree on an arbitrator, the matter will be decided by a panel of three arbitrators. We will each choose one arbitrator, who need not have any particular professional background, and our two arbitrators together will appoint the third arbitrator who must be a family law professional as specified above.

2. If we use a single arbitrator, we will pay the cost of arbitration from marital funds, if available, and if marital funds are not available, we will each be responsible for half the cost of the arbitration. If we use a panel of three arbitrators, each of us will pay the fees of the arbitrator we appoint. The fees of the third arbitrator will be paid from marital funds, if available, and if marital funds are not available, we will each be responsible for half the fees of the third arbitrator and other costs of arbitration.

3. We are each entitled to representation in arbitration by an attorney of our choice. Attorney fees will be paid from marital funds, if available, and if marital funds are not available, each party will be responsible for his or her own attorney's fees.

4. **Rules and powers of the arbitrator(s).** The arbitration will be conducted under rules to be agreed upon by the arbitrator(s) and the parties, but if there is no consensus, the rules will be determined by the arbitrator(s). In any event, the parties agree they will adopt and apply the Nolo Supplementary Family Arbitration Rules, a copy of which is attached to this agreement as Exhibit A. The arbitrator(s) will have the power to interpret the terms of this agreement, decide questions of their own jurisdiction, and settle disputes arising between the parties. The arbitrator(s) will not have the power to alter, modify or terminate any provision of this agreement.

5. **Arbitration is binding and final.** The decision of the arbitrator(s) will be binding and final, not subject to review in any court. We each understand that by agreeing to binding arbitration, we are choosing arbitration as the sole remedy for any dispute between us, and we each expressly give up our right to file a lawsuit or family law proceeding in any court against one another, or to request a court to resolve any dispute between us, except to compel arbitration or enforce the decision of an arbitrator. We understand that this means we are giving up the right to trial by a court or by a jury. To whatever extent

the law does not allow any issue between us to be decided by binding arbitration, we agree to submit such matters to nonbinding arbitration before submitting the issue to any court.

10. Severability, governing law, interpretation, modification

A. Severability

Each clause of this agreement is separate and divisible from the others. Should any court or arbitrator refuse to enforce one or more clauses, in whole or in part, the remainder of such clauses, and the remainder of the entire agreement, are to remain valid and in full force.

B. Entire agreement and consideration

This document sets forth our entire agreement. It supersedes any and all other agreements, either oral or in writing, between us regarding our mutual rights and obligations arising from our relationship. The promises of each of us are consideration for the promises of the other.

C. Binding effect

Once this agreement takes effect, as described in paragraph 3, it will become binding on us and on our respective heirs, executors and administrators.

D. Governing law and interpretation

The validity and interpretation of this agreement will be governed in accordance with the laws of the State of Texas, in which we both permanently resided at the time this agreement was signed. It will be interpreted fairly, simply, and not strictly for or against either party. Copies of this signed agreement may be submitted and accepted into evidence in place of the original in any proceeding to enforce or interpret the terms of this agreement.

We do not wish to have our mutual rights and obligations changed by the fact that we may choose to reside in another state some day, so we agree that the previous paragraph will apply no matter where we might live at any time during our marriage.

E. Modification

This agreement may be modified or revoked only by written agreement, signed by both of us.

Signatures

We have each read this agreement carefully and are signing it freely, voluntarily, and with full understanding of its meaning after having obtained all the advice we each, individually, feel is appropriate.

This agreement was delivered to Chris Brown by Jamie Jones on (date)

Dated: _____   _____

                                  Chris Brown

This agreement was delivered to Jamie Jones by Chris Brown on (date)

Dated: _____   _____

                                  Jamie Jones

Attachments

Exhibit A   Nolo Supplementary Family Arbitration Rules

CHAPTER

2

Doing your own basic Couples Contract

This chapter discusses the basic Couples Contract in detail, starting with exactly how you go about doing your own, followed by a template of the basic contract in section B with a discussion of each clause, and a discussion of lifestyle agreements in section C.

It is *very* easy to do your own Couples Contract and well worth the little effort it will take. All you have to do is check some boxes and fill in some blanks. When you make this agreement, you gain some vital advantages:

- Loving commitment to a lasting relationship
- Build successful problem-solving into your relationship
- Avoid surprises if you should ever move to another state
- Make sure your relationship never ends up in court

No changes in legal relationships. The basic Couples Contract does not alter your legal relationships, apart from agreeing to use mediation and arbitration to resolve disputes, if any ever arise, instead of going to court. For everything else, it simply adopts the law of your home state to govern your rights and duties, just as if you married without an agreement. This allows you to get all the positive advantages of a Couples Contract without having to discuss money and property matters—unless, that is, your situation makes it important that you do so right away, or you believe as we do that the ability to discuss money and be clear about financial matters will help build a foundation for a lasting relationship.

Married or pre-marriage couples. These instructions are for couples who are either married or soon will be.[1]

Unmarried couples[2] should start in chapter 7 and return here as directed.

Going beyond the basic

The basic Couples Contract creates a framework within which you can tailor your financial relationships or add faith-based features, which is something you can do either now, in the future, or never. Extensions to the basic Couples Contract are discussed in chapters 3–7.

---

[1] In those few states (3 or 4) that provide for substantially equal rights (and duties) for same-sex couples who register a Civil Union or Domestic Partnership, this applies to you, too.

[2] For purposes of the Couples Contract, the legal issues facing unmarried couples are the same, no matter what their sexual orientation.

A. How to prepare your own basic agreement

Section B is a template that you should follow closely to make your own basic agreement. It offers a few options that you will select to make it fit your situation. Clauses are displayed on the right page, and each clause has comments on the left page that explains what is being done and how to choose options.

Three methods. There are three methods you can use to prepare your own contract:

1) **Low-tech.** Use a typewriter to create your contract, following the template and instructions in section B.

2) **Easiest.** Forget the template; just use the Basic Couples Contract kit on the CD. Open the Couples Contract form in the free Adobe Reader program (see Appendix D), check boxes and fill in blanks with your names and other information, print it on quality paper or vellum, and *voila!* you're done.

3) **Best-looking.** Use your favorite word processor. Go to the chapter 2 folder on the CD, and open the Basic Couples Contract file. Follow the instructions in section B to create your own Couples Contract. Use whatever font you like and format to make it look the way you want, then print it on quality paper or vellum.

Next, follow instructions in chapters 8 and 9. Essentially, this means you create two short, simple documents—one is a waiver of attorneys and the other explains what the contract does in simple terms. You can do them any of the three ways described above, but for these utilitarian documents, the easiest method is probably good enough. Finally, you need someone to witness your signing of the documents. That's it; you're done.

Typing or word processing. Be sure to change the names in the sample documents to your own names. Use Find or Replace commands to make sure you have found and changed names in every location. Use your names one way throughout the agreement and all other documents or attachments. For example, do not use Jamie Jones, Jamie J. Jones, and J. J. Jones in various places; pick one and stick with it. And, while this is not a legal requirement, it would be good form to name the parties in the same order from start to finish—first Chris, then Jamie— to help keep things straight in everyone's mind.

Wherever there are options, choose which you will use. Delete all check boxes and unused text—just keep the text you want to use.

B.   Template for the basic Couples Contract

The template for the basic Couples Contract is on the right side, discussion and tips are on the left. In the template, we put check boxes next to clauses that are optional and depend either on your particular situation or preference.

Heading, introduction and parties[3]

Title. For a heading, we used "Relationship Affirmations and Agreement," but you can call it anything you like that isn't misleading. You could just put the names of the parties at the top, or Lasting Relationship Agreement, Relationship Agreement, Our Vows, or It's a Deal! This is more a matter of taste and tone, as your agreement's legal meaning will be found in the text.

Parties. We name the parties with pleasant language that gives your agreement a loving, personal feeling. The nice tone is continued by using first names of the parties from this point forward. In our sample agreement, we use the names Chris Brown and Jamie Jones to represent any couple. You, of course, will substitute your own names throughout.

1.   Purpose. This section states in general terms what you intend to accomplish in your agreement. Items A through E describe very constructive features, so should be used in every agreement. Enter your home state (where at least one of you resides when you sign the agreement) in clause D. If you tailor your agreement as described in chapters 5, 6 or 7, you should use any of the optional purpose clauses that are relevant to whatever features you add to your agreement.

2.   Commitments. This clause states what the law calls the "fiduciary duty" that all couples *should* owe one another, but it is not completely clear that they do for all couples under the laws of all states, so it is worth making this clear in your Couples Contract.

Getting married. The fiduciary duty would not normally apply until *after* you marry, but the wording here means you are adopting the highest standard toward one another even while making the Couples Contract.

Married people. You might live in a state where this duty is not clearly defined, or someday move to such a state. With the Couples Contract, the duty you owe each other is clear no matter where you live, either now or later.

---

[3] In South Carolina, these words must appear on the first page in underlined capital letters: NOTICE: THIS CONTRACT IS SUBJECT TO ARBITRATION PURSUANT TO CODE OF LAWS OF SOUTH CAROLINA, 1976, TITLE 15, CHAPTER 48.

Relationship Affirmations and Agreement
of Chris Brown and Jamie Jones

In loving anticipation of a lasting relationship, this agreement is made between Chris Brown and Jamie Jones, called by our first names in this agreement.

1. **Purpose.** The purpose of our agreement is:

    A.   To affirm our commitment to one another and to a lasting relationship based upon trust, mutual respect, affection and friendship.

    B.   To establish principles that will help us resolve personal issues that might threaten to weaken our relationship, should any ever arise.

    C.   To entirely and forever remove our relationship from the adversarial court system by committing to resolve disagreements of any nature that might arise between us, that we cannot resolve privately, by mediation or arbitration.

    D.   To govern our relationship rights and obligations according to the laws of _____, except as modified by this agreement.

    E.   To create stability and predictability by governing our relationship rights and obligations according to the terms of this agreement no matter where we might reside in the future.

[optional clauses to use if you add variations from chapters 5–7]

☐ To define and clarify our assets and debts

☐ To define our mutual rights and obligations with respect to financial matters

☐ To define our mutual rights and obligations with respect to parenting matters

☐ To provide for children of a prior relationship

☐ To set forth our rights and obligations should we separate or divorce

2. Commitments

In the making of this agreement and forever after, we affirm our close and confidential relationship and commit ourselves to mutual respect, openness, honesty, and the highest standards of good faith and fair dealing with one another in all matters, putting each other's best interests equal to our own.

Unmarried people. This clause is essential! Without it, you are strangers under the law who owe little duty to one another unless you can prove in court that a confidential relationship exists, so make it clear in your Couples Contract.

Read more. An article about the fiduciary duty in various states appears in the Legal Briefs folder on the CD where you can read about it in more detail.

3. Effective date and duration

Before marriage. If you are not married yet but intend to marry in the near future, state that your agreement becomes effective when you marry.

After marriage, or unmarried. If you are making this agreement after you have already married, or if you are unmarried, your agreement should become effective when signed by both parties.

Duration. Your basic agreement is going to stay in effect indefinitely because you want the positive and constructive features of the basic contract to last a lifetime.

4. Principles for a lasting relationship

Be sure to read chapter 2C, which discusses the purpose and possibilities for this section—in short, to remind you to focus on the positive features of your relationship and to introduce ideas that might someday help you get more smoothly through the kinds of problems most couples face, sooner or later.

This is a new concept in both contracts and couples counseling, so there's plenty of room for variation here. This section is not meant to be a binding legal agreement, so we are not as concerned about precision of language as in other parts of the agreement. You are free to add other ideas you think might someday be useful, and you can substitute other resources for the books and tapes we used in our example. There's a lot of material out there; start with our list in Appendix C, then hunt around or ask counselors and others who are in a position to know.

It might look like there's not much to this section (which is good because it won't get in anyone's way), but don't underestimate the value of planting the idea that a relationship takes some effort; that there are things you can do to promote friendship and affection; and, some specific ideas for where to start. Someday you might be glad you remembered it.

5. Parenting

Enter the name of your home state (where at least one of you resides when you sign the agreement). This must be the same state that you name in clause 10D.

3. Effective date and duration of agreement

☐ Our agreement will become effective when we marry. If we do not marry, it will be of no effect.

☐ Our agreement will become effective once it has been signed by both parties.

Once it takes effect, our agreement will remain in effect indefinitely, or until we sign a written agreement to modify or revoke it.

4. Principles for a lasting relationship

We believe that a lasting relationship is based upon trust, mutual respect, affection and friendship. It is our goal to preserve and reinforce these features in our union.

We know that a lasting relationship sometimes requires an intentional effort, that reinforcing positive features is essential, and that practices learned from couples counseling have an excellent record of success.

If ever circumstances arise that threaten to undermine our mutual regard, we agree to make an effort to reinforce positive qualities in our relationship and resolve issues that weaken them.

We agree that if one of us requests it, we will set aside some quiet time to discuss our relationship together and seek ways to reinforce the positive features that are vital to our well-being as a couple. We will look for information in books, tapes or videos, starting with **[Note: the following are our examples, but you can insert here any resources you favor]** Dr. John Gottman's material on *The Seven Principles for Making Marriages Work*, and we will look at Dr. Gary Chapman's material about *The Five Love Languages*. We will also consider going to conciliation, or to a couples workshop, or to a couples coach or counselor.

5. Parenting

We agree that, except as modified by this agreement, our rights and duties as parents of any children born to or legally adopted by us will be governed by the laws of the State of _____.

6. Money, property and financial matters

In this basic agreement, you are adopting the law of your home state (the same state named in clause 10D) to govern all marital affairs, with one exception—your agreement to use mediation and arbitration rather than courts to resolve disputes, if any arise. Be sure to review chapter 5 to see if you are one of those couples who would be better off tailoring financial relationships and how to do it.

This clause will help keep your financial rights and duties to each other from changing if you move to another state. However, if ever you plan to move, visit a family law attorney in the new state, or use methods discussed in chapter 4G, to find out how things work where you are moving, then review your agreement. Ideally, you'll do this before you move, but certainly soon after you arrive. Later, you can modify your agreement if you prefer any legal features in your new state.

7. Disclosures

Enter the name of your home state. Because the basic agreement does not alter financial rights and responsibilities, you can get by without making financial disclosures to one another. However, if you decide to do financial tailoring along the lines discussed in chapter 6, you are *required* to make full financial disclosure.

Taking the high road. Sharing financial information and having discussions about your finances and spending habits is a good thing to do as it helps build a solid foundation for your future, so we urge you to do financial disclosure in every case. Most couples counselors and financial planners agree.

How to do it. Whether you do disclosure because you know it is right or because you have to do it, follow the instructions in chapter 5F and replace this entire section 7 with language that is provided there.

8. Representation and drafting

Indicate who prepared the agreement: one or the other of you, or both working together. While not necessary, it is better if you work on it together. The agreement is all about being a couple so it only makes sense to do it together and, besides, doing it together strengthens your agreement by making it more clear that you both signed it voluntarily and with full knowledge of its contents.

Being represented by independent counsel can be waived (given up), as we have you do here. This does *not* mean you can't get advice from an attorney or anyone else. In fact, we think that, depending on the nature of your questions, it can be useful to get information and advice from a family law attorney or,

6. Money, property and financial matters

Except as modified by this agreement, we agree that all of our mutual rights and obligations with respect to our financial affairs, including our income, debts, and property, will be governed by the laws of _____ , no matter where we might live in the future.

7. Disclosures

Our agreement does not alter financial rights and duties under _____ law, therefore:

I, Chris, am sufficiently aware of Jamie's financial circumstances and I freely and voluntarily give up the right to formal written disclosure or any other information about Jamie's finances.

I, Jamie, am sufficiently aware of Chris's financial circumstances and I freely and voluntarily give up the right to formal written disclosure or any other information about Chris's finances.

8. Representation and drafting

☐ Chris and Jamie drafted this agreement together, jointly.

☐ This agreement was primarily drafted by ☐ Chris. ☐ Jamie.

I, Chris, understand that I have the right to be represented by an independent attorney in the negotiation and preparation of this agreement and I have sufficient funds to retain an attorney for this purpose if I want one. Nonetheless, I choose not to be represented. I understand the terms of this agreement and have had ample opportunity to seek the advice of an attorney or any other kind of advisor. I have read this agreement carefully and have received as much advice as I wish to receive. I freely and voluntarily choose to sign it without being represented by an attorney at this time.

I, Jamie, understand that I have the right to be represented by an independent attorney in the negotiation and preparation of this agreement and I have sufficient funds to retain an attorney for this purpose if I want one. Nonetheless, I choose not to be represented. I understand the terms of this agreement and have had ample opportunity to seek the advice of an attorney or any other kind of advisor. I have read this agreement carefully and have received as much advice as I wish to receive. I freely and voluntarily choose to sign it without being represented by an attorney at this time.

depending on the subject and your questions, other professionals such as financial planners, tax accountants, couples counselors or clergy.

9. Resolution of disputes—mediation and arbitration

Read chapter 1B(4). This section alone is worth the small effort it takes to make this agreement. It replaces the conflict-oriented court system with something much more suitable for the resolution of family disputes—mediation and arbitration. You need to go into some detail about how things should be done and who pays for it, so this section is longer than others in the basic agreement. Mediation and arbitration are known as *alternative dispute resolution*, or ADR. The laws and judges in most states encourage ADR so a judge will almost certainly send you packing out of her courtroom if anyone tries to head there to avoid arbitration.

You can use ADR methods informally at any time, even for relatively minor disagreements; people do it all the time. They might go to a friend, relative, clergy or other advisor and say, "We have this problem; please help us figure out what to do." This is a form of ADR. People even arbitrate minor disputes using a coin toss instead of a human being as arbitrator. Any form of ADR beats going to court.

Mediation

Mediator qualifications. A mediator who is a family law professional in your area will know the law and can advise you *during mediation* about how the laws apply to your situation or when someone's expectations are outside the bounds. Most family mediations will benefit from this kind of expertise. However, if the primary focus of mediation is possible reconciliation or parenting, a professional marriage counselor could be more effective than a family law attorney. In that case, when it comes time to mediate, you can (perhaps should) agree to use a different kind of mediator. However, if legal issues come up during mediation, you might wish you had gone with the attorney-mediator in the first place.

Arbitration

Three-arbitrator panel. Described in clause 9B(1), this is a proven method with a long history. One of the advantages, depending upon whom you choose, is that the dispute doesn't necessarily have to be decided by a total stranger.

The Nolo Supplementary Family Arbitration Rules. Arbitration is typically, though not always, conducted under a specific set of rules. Few existing sets of rules are designed for family cases, so we created our own supplemental set. The

9. Resolution of disputes—mediation and arbitration

It is our desire to remove our relationship entirely and forever from the adversarial court system and to resolve any dispute that might arise between us or under this agreement by mediation and arbitration.

A. Mediation

1. If we are unable to resolve any dispute ourselves or with counseling, then we each agree to make a reasonable good-faith effort to resolve the matter in mediation. On the written request of either party we will within thirty days submit our dispute to mediation with a mediator agreed upon by both of us. Unless we agree otherwise, our mediator must be a family law attorney who specializes in family law mediation in the state named in clause 10D. If we are unable to agree on a mediator, we will each choose one person to make a choice on our behalf, and those two persons together will appoint our mediator. We will participate in mediation in good faith and pay the cost of mediation from marital funds, if available, and if marital funds are not available, we will each be responsible for half the cost of such mediation.

2. We are each entitled to representation in mediation by an attorney of our choice. Attorney fees will be ☐ borne by each party separately ☐ paid from marital funds, if available, and if marital funds are not available, each party will be responsible for his or her own attorney's fees.

B. Arbitration

1. In the event that mediation does not resolve all issues within a reasonable number of sessions, then on the written request of either of us, **WE WILL SUBMIT THE MATTER TO BINDING ARBITRATION** within ninety days. The arbitrator will be agreed upon by both of us, but must be a family law professional in the state named in clause 10D: either an attorney who specializes in mediation or arbitration, or a retired family court judge. If we are unable to agree on an arbitrator, the matter will be decided by a panel of three arbitrators. We will each choose one arbitrator, who need not have any particular professional background, and our two arbitrators together will appoint the third arbitrator who must be a family law professional as specified above.

2. If we use a single arbitrator, we will pay the cost of arbitration from marital funds, if available, and if marital funds are not available, we will each be responsible for half the cost of the arbitration. If we use a panel of three arbitrators, each of us will pay the fees of the arbitrator we appoint. The fees of the third arbitrator will be paid from marital funds, if available, and if marital funds are not available, we will each be responsible for half the fees of the third arbitrator and other costs of arbitration.

Nolo Supplementary Family Arbitration Rules add essential features to cover two situations: (1) emergencies in the period before arbitrators have been appointed, and (2) events that might arise after arbitration has been concluded. These are discussed in more detail in Appendix B, where the Nolo Rules are printed.

Must be attached. A copy of the Nolo Rules must be attached to your agreement as Exhibit A, so if you ever need arbitration in the future, the arbitrators will know how to proceed. A copy of these rules can be found on the companion CD so you can print it out. If you don't have a computer, simply make a copy of the rules from Appendix B and attach that as Exhibit A.

Binding arbitration.[4] Arbitration will be binding on all issues, but courts in any state will be willing to review child custody and child support decisions, and possibly spousal support too. However, the last sentence of clause 9B(5) means that the couple must first go through arbitration on *every* issue, whether the state courts will regard it as binding or not. This way, couples *must* proceed in a healthier forum before they can get to court, and that is a *very* good thing. We believe the majority of couples will settle all issues if they feel they've had their say and a fair shake, especially since courts give strong weight to an arbitrator's decision. This makes the Couples Contract very much worth doing.

Read more. An article about the enforceability of agreements to submit to binding arbitration can be found in the Legal Briefs folder on the companion CD.

How to choose wisely

Not just any mediator or arbitrator will do—you need someone with knowledge, experience and a good record. Make sure that family mediation or arbitration is the primary focus of the attorney's practice and litigation is minimal or zero. Ask how many cases they have successfully concluded. If you move to a distant state, your problem will be to find a professional who knows the law of your home state, the basis of your agreement. You'll want to look for someone who promises to brush up on that law, or you might travel to your home state for the time it takes, or import a mediator or arbitrator rather than go yourselves.

10. Severability, governing law, interpretation, modification

A. Your agreement may include some clauses, like the one about relationship principles, that are not intended to be enforced. This makes it very important to make it clear that each part of your agreement is separate (severable) and

---

[4] In clause 9B(1), "we will submit the matter to binding arbitration" appears in bold, underlined capitals to meet statutory requirements of a few states that want to make sure this gets noticed.

3.   We are each entitled to representation in arbitration by an attorney of our choice. Attorney fees will be ☐ borne by each party separately. ☐ paid from marital funds, if available, and if marital funds are not available, each party will be responsible for his or her own attorney's fees.

4.   **Rules and powers of the arbitrator(s).** The arbitration will be conducted under rules to be agreed upon by the arbitrator(s) and the parties, but if there is no consensus, the rules will be determined by the arbitrator(s). In any event, the parties agree they will adopt and apply the Nolo Supplementary Family Arbitration Rules, a copy of which is attached to this agreement as Exhibit A. The arbitrator(s) will have the power to interpret the terms of this agreement, decide questions of their own jurisdiction, and settle disputes arising between the parties. The arbitrator(s) will not have the power to alter, modify or terminate any provision of this agreement.

5.   **Arbitration is binding and final.** The decision of the arbitrator(s) will be binding and final, not subject to review in any court. We each understand that by agreeing to binding arbitration, we are choosing arbitration as the sole remedy for any dispute between us, and we each expressly give up our right to file a lawsuit or family law proceeding in any court against one another, or to request a court to resolve any dispute between us, except to compel arbitration or enforce the decision of an arbitrator. We understand that this means we are giving up the right to trial by a court or by a jury. To whatever extent the law does not allow any issue between us to be decided by binding arbitration, we agree to submit such matters to nonbinding arbitration before submitting the issue to any court.

[Optional]

6.   If an action is required to enforce the use of binding arbitration required by this agreement, or the decision of an arbitrator, the costs and expenses of the prevailing party in such judicial proceeding, including, but not limited to, his or her reasonable attorney's fees, will be paid by the unsuccessful party.

10. Severability, governing law, interpretation, modification

A. Severability

Each clause of this agreement is separate and divisible from the others. Should any court or arbitrator refuse to enforce one or more clauses, in whole or in part, the remainder of such clauses, and the remainder of the entire agreement, are to remain valid and in full force.

independent, so that enforceable clauses will stay in force even if some other parts are found to be not enforceable. Don't leave this one out.

B. This clause says that this is now the only agreement between you, replacing all others and any oral understandings you might have had.

Caution! If you have other agreements between you, written or oral, either write them into this agreement or forget about them, because anything you leave out will not be enforceable. It wouldn't hurt to formally cancel any prior agreements by writing "CANCELED" along with your initials across the pages. Likewise, be careful that you don't overlook a clause like this in the fine print of any future agreement you might make between you, as any terms of this Couples Contract that are inconsistent with the new agreement will then be canceled.

C. This requires your heirs, as well as the executor of your will or the administrator of your estate to comply with the terms of the agreement.

D. The first paragraph establishes the laws of your home state as the governing authority for your Couples Contract, while the second paragraph states your intention to have your rights and duties governed by those laws even if you move to another state. This will certainly work for the financial rights and duties between you, but child custody and support will always be determined by the laws of whatever state a child lives in, no matter what your agreement says. Similarly, the rules for *intestate succession*—what happens if someone dies without a will—are not affected by this clause, so be sure to make wills no matter where you live.

- "Home state" is the state in which at least one of you permanently resides when you sign your agreement.
- Note. While we don't recommend it, it is sometimes possible to choose the laws of a state you do not live in to govern your contract.

Read more. An article about choosing the governing law of a state you do not live in appears in the Legal Briefs folder on the CD.

E. The modification clause makes clear that your agreement cannot be changed or terminated except by written agreement signed by both of you.

B. Entire agreement and consideration

This document sets forth our entire agreement. It supersedes any and all other agreements, either oral or in writing, between us regarding our mutual rights and obligations arising from our relationship. The promises of each of us are consideration for the promises of the other.

C. Binding effect

Once this agreement takes effect, as described in paragraph 3, it will become binding on us and on our respective heirs, executors and administrators.

D. Governing law and interpretation

The validity and interpretation of this agreement will be governed in accordance with the laws of the State of _____, in which (Chris/Jamie/we both) permanently resided at the time this agreement was signed. It will be interpreted fairly, simply, and not strictly for or against either party. Copies of this signed agreement may be submitted and accepted into evidence in place of the original in any proceeding to enforce or interpret the terms of this agreement.

We do not wish to have our mutual rights and obligations changed by the fact that we may choose to reside in another state some day, so we agree that the previous paragraph will apply no matter where we might live at any time during our marriage.

E. Modification

This agreement may be modified or revoked only by written agreement, signed by both of us.

Signatures—date but don't sign yet

Above each signature line, enter the date you hand each other the final draft of the agreement and the Explanation of Agreement (chapter 8), but do *not* actually sign it yet. The actual signing takes place later, as described in chapter 9C. Take some time to read the agreement very carefully, every word, and clarify any parts you don't understand or find confusing. If you want to get advice or discuss the agreement with someone, this is when you should call a family law attorney (chapter 3B). There should be at least seven full days between the date you first received the final agreement and the date you actually sign it. This is to give you time to read, think, and get advice. In some cases, more time will be required (see chapter 9B).

Attachments. Indicate what documents are attached to your agreement. Every agreement will have Exhibit A, the Nolo Rules. Schedules 1 and 2 will be attached if you did financial disclosure as discussed in chapter 5F.

Signatures

We have each read this agreement carefully and are signing it freely, voluntarily, and with full understanding of its meaning after having obtained all the advice we each, individually, feel is appropriate.

This agreement was delivered to Chris by Jamie on ____(date)____

Dated: _____   _____
                                                    Chris Brown

This agreement was delivered to Jamie by Chris on ____(date)____

Dated: _____   _____
                                                    Jamie Jones

Attachments

Exhibit A   Nolo Supplementary Family Arbitration Rules
☐ Schedule 1   Chris's financial disclosure
☐ Schedule 2   Jamie's financial disclosure

C. Lifestyle agreements

Some couples want to agree in detail how they plan to live together: everything from whether they'll have children to what part of income they'll invest to who will do dishes or agreements about fidelity and sexual practices. Taken as a group, these are called *lifestyle* agreements, and courts don't want anything to do with them. You can't get a court to order someone to do housework or be thrifty or assess damages against a spouse who refuses. They are generally not enforceable.

Traditional lawyers regard lifestyle agreements as trivial and recommend leaving them out of marital contracts because they fear such clauses might undermine the enforceability of the rest of the agreement if a judge decides they were a major consideration for making the agreement in the first place.

We disagree, at least in part. Lifestyle agreements are not trivial to the couple or they would not have taken the trouble to work them out. Including them in the Couples Contract should not make other parts unenforceable because clause 10A states that unenforceable portions do not affect parts of the agreement that are enforceable. Another point is that the Couples Contract requires that all disputes be settled by mediation or arbitration, so questions of enforceability will be decided by an arbitrator, not a judge, and it is at least possible that an arbitrator will consider lifestyle agreements in ways that a court would not.

We think it is good to discuss ideas and expectations for how you want to live together, and if it pleases you to write things down in the form of an agreement, go ahead. However, we think it best *not* to put details about your preferred lifestyle in your Couples Contract.

Separate document preferred. There are advantages to putting lifestyle agreements in a separate contract or letter that you both sign rather than putting them in your Couples Contract. The first consideration is flexibility: people and circumstances change, so you will probably want to adjust your lifestyle agreements from time to time, but if they are part of your Couples Contract, this means going through a formal modification (chapter 9G), which takes some effort and bother. If they are in a separate document, you can simply tear it up and write another. The other consideration is a matter of tone and privacy. When you sign your Couples Contract, you'll have a witness to your agreement who will need to see it (chapter 9C) and you might even make the signing into a bit of a ceremony for close friends and relatives who will probably be curious to see your agreement. If your Couples Contract involves real estate or creditors, at some point even strangers might need to examine it. Does it feel comfortable for you to have other people read your lifestyle agreements? If not, you'd be better off putting them in a separate letter or contract which is kept entirely private between the two of you. On the other hand, if these are things you want your arbitrator to consider and decide, you might favor putting them in your Couples Contract.

How to do it. If you decide you *must* have lifestyle clauses in your Couples Contract, you would insert a new section 6 into your basic agreement, like this:

6. Lifestyle agreements

We understand that lifestyle agreements might not be enforceable in a court of law, but we wish to include them here in order to remind ourselves of our plans for how we want to live together. This section is not the consideration for our consent to any other portion of our agreement.

A.   [insert your agreements . . .]

Of course, you'll have to renumber the old section 6 and sections that follow.

Don't mention sex. Do not, under any circumstances, include expectations about your sex life or refer to a party as "lover" in your Couples Contract because courts are hypersensitive to sex and can't be trusted to react reasonably to it in a legal setting. Yes, your agreement requires arbitration, not court; but if the validity of the agreement as a whole were attacked in court, a judge could possibly interpret your agreement as inherently and basically a contract for sex, which is either a crime or at least against public policy, so the whole thing could be thrown out, arbitration clause and all. Not likely, but why take the chance?

Open marriages.[5] Some couples are committed but agree to an open relationship, preferring this to an assumed exclusivity that could lead them to regard outside relationships as lying in cheating. Some agree that neither party is obliged to account to the other for how they spend their money, their time, or the company they keep. Others might specify one boy's night out, one girl's night out, and one date night with each other, but for nights out the rule is "don't ask, don't tell." Yet others might agree to be sexually exclusive in general, but when one is traveling, some latitude is understood. It is always a good idea to agree explicitly that you will not have unprotected sex outside the relationship. Whatever your arrangement, it is essential to clearly understand the boundaries of your relationship, but for all the reasons mentioned above, you should put the terms of your open relationship in a side agreement, not in your Couples Contract.

---

[5] Thanks to financial advisor Bert Whitehead, MBA, JD, for information on open marriage.

D. Completing your agreement

Once you've prepared your basic Couples Contract, if you are not adding more terms (chapters 3–7) at this time, go on to chapters 8 and 9 to take steps that will make your contract enforceable in any state. Skip past comments there that are intended for people who added financial or other features. Following the simple instructions, you'll add two brief supporting documents and get someone to witness your signatures and sign a declaration about it.

E. Legal validity of the Couples Contract

Whether a contract is *valid* is really a question of whether it is *enforceable*. If one party tries to enforce the contract, will a court or arbitrator provide a remedy? For contracts between two individuals, the rules about validity, and limitations placed on such contracts, vary from state to state.

Marital and premarital relationships. If you are married or getting married, don't worry about validity: just follow the steps in this book and your Couples Contract will be valid in any state.

Civil union or domestic partnership. The states that have domestic partnership or civil union for same-sex couples likewise recognize contracts entered into between prospective or existing partners.

Unmarried couples. Thirty-six states recognize your right to make agreements about your affairs, so long as your sexual relationship is not a prominent part of the consideration; so, best not to mention sex at all. Also, don't agree never to marry, as that could be seen as being against public policy. However, in 11 states, there is no mention about cohabitation agreements either way, and in Georgia, validity is a bit dicey, though not a lost cause. **Caution.** There's cause for concern in Illinois and Delaware, where they seem to assume that any contract between cohabitants contemplates illicit sex and is therefore not enforceable as a matter of public policy. If you live in one of these states, get advice from a family law attorney about how best to define your financial rights (see chapter 3B).

Read more. An article about the enforceability of premarital agreements and cohabitation agreements in various states can be found in the Legal Briefs folder on the companion CD.

CHAPTER

3

Getting your Couples Contract to do more

As valuable as the Couples Contract is for every couple, there's much more that can be done. For some couples, doing more will be attractive, while for others it will be essential! Every couple should read chapters 3–6 (and chapter 7 for unmarried couples) so you will at least be aware of the possibilities.

Once you depart from the basic contract and start introducing additional features, you also introduce a degree of complexity that requires more information, thought and—most important—discussions between the two of you. For some issues you might also want professional advice or other assistance (see section B below).

"Tailoring" your financial relationships means changing them by agreement from what the laws of your state provide. So, before you can consider possible advantages of doing this, you need to know more about how your state governs the affairs of couples who have no agreements. This is discussed in chapter 4, and actual tailoring with examples and instructions is in chapter 5. Financial tailoring for unmarried couples is discussed in chapter 7.

For those of you who are members of a faith community that is very important to your lives, you can consider the advantages of incorporating some faith-based features into your agreement (see chapter 6).

A. Working together

A major goal of your agreement is to safeguard mutual respect, trust and affection in your relationship, so we know you'll keep that in mind when you work on it.

There's not much to disagree about in the basic agreement (chapter 2), which has only positive and constructive things in it, so your discussions should be easy and you probably won't need advice about how to work together.

If you tailor your financial relationships, or one of you wants faith-based features, you might run into things that can be a challenge to discuss. So what? You don't have to agree about everything to be in love or stay together forever, but you do have to find ways to accommodate different points of view. Loving couples sometimes have issues that are difficult to deal with. If this happens, it doesn't mean you don't love each other, but it might mean you should work with someone skilled to help find a successful conclusion that satisfies both of you. You are two

Checklist for an extended agreement

☐   1.   Read this book and discuss ideas in it together

☐   2.   Decide if you want to do the basic agreement (chapter 2) first, or wait until you add extended features and do it all at once.

> **Note.** Unmarried couples who don't plan to marry should read chapter 7 now, then continue.

☐   3.   Decide if you want to tailor your financial relationships (chapter 5)
> ☐ If yes, do financial disclosure (chapter 5F)

☐   4.   Decide if you want faith-based features (chapter 6)

☐   5.   Consider getting advice or independent counsel (chapter 3B)

☐   6.   Assemble your agreement (chapter 3C)

☐   7.   Prepare two additional documents (chapter 8)

☐   8.   Present each other with final agreement and explanation (9B)

☐   9.   Wait at least seven days (9B), sign agreement and waiver (9C)

☐   10.   Notarize both of your signatures and that of your witness (9C)

☐   11.   Follow through (chapter 9E)

different people, so from time to time you're going to run into things you don't agree on. Here are some suggestions in case this turns out to be one of those times.

Allow plenty of time. Don't put yourselves in a situation where you have to rush. Making an extended Couples Contract might take some thought and discussion with your partner before you draft and sign it. This is an important document, so you should give it the time it deserves. In cases where courts have invalidated a premarital agreement, it was often a factor that the agreement was signed in a hurry or under pressure.

- If you just do the basic agreement, allow a few weeks.
- If you tailor financial relationships (chapter 5), you should allow a few months or more.

Giving yourselves plenty of time will take the pressure off, keep you relaxed, and help make it better and more meaningful.

If you feel you could use a little help or a sounding board for your ideas, don't hesitate to call a reliable family law attorney to discuss your situation (see section B below). Also consider talking with a financial planner or personal advisor such as mentors, family members or close friends for their input and suggestions.

Back to basics. If you get stuck discussing any of the variations, just do the ones you agree on or drop variations all together and just do the basic agreement. That gets you most of the advantages of the Couples Contract and you can always modify it later (chapter 9G) whenever you reach agreement on other terms. So there's no pressure—you don't have to agree on everything, or anything beyond the basics.

Time and place. Arrange to meet at a convenient time and place specifically to discuss your agreement—a time when you can both be rested, relaxed and free of interruption and a place good for quiet but concentrated conversation. Don't make it a marathon, but set a reasonable amount of time aside and plan to meet again, as often as it takes, until you get through to the end. No rush, no pressure.

Reflection. Before you meet, and especially between meetings, take time to dig into your own thoughts and feelings and what you understand to be the thoughts and feelings of your partner. You are particularly trying to understand the interests of both parties, starting with yourself.

Discuss interests rather than what you want. An interest is not the same as what you want—it is *why* you want what you want, which you might possibly not be aware of at first. For example, putting funds into a joint account might be what you *want*, and you know you want it, but your *interests* might be to feel safe and secure and to be treated fairly. When you just say what you want, you either get it or you don't, which makes it seem like your partner is trying to deny you something if he/she has different ideas. Interests are easier to discuss in ways that might uncover options that get what you want in a way you hadn't thought of.

Speak clearly. Don't expect your partner to read your mind or guess your feelings. It's up to you to understand what you think and feel and then communicate this clearly. Speak kindly from the place where you feel affection. Don't be pushy or keep repeating yourself, but do make sure you are being understood by asking your partner to say back to you what he/she understands you to mean.

Listen attentively. Pay attention and, especially, look like you're paying attention. Listen to understand what is meant and what your partner is feeling.

Don't interrupt; wait until your partner is through saying his/her piece. Don't get distracted by your own thoughts or fidget or look around. Confirm what was said by saying in your own words what you understand the other person to be saying and feeling, then ask, "Is that right?" "Do you mean . . . ?"

Take notes. Keep a journal with notes of each meeting. Write down the things you agree about and keep expanding the list. Write down things you don't agree about and try to break them down to see if you can agree on parts of those subjects.

Resolving differences. Once you are both satisfied that you understand each other on a certain point, try to go behind the point to your interests—why you want what you want. Take time off from your discussion and return after you've both thought about what was said and had a chance to think about your interests. Look for new ideas that might address your mutual interests in a different way.

Never forget your first priority. Your relationship is your first priority. The whole point of the Couples Contract is to protect your mutual affection and regard, so it would be sad and ironic (not to mention revealing) if discussing it undermined that goal. Don't let frustration make disagreement sound like anger or lack of respect. Avoid sarcasm. It's okay to disagree, but not okay to undermine your relationship along the way. Stay calm, stay loving, and at all times be kind.

If you get stuck. If you both understand each other and your mutual interests and haven't found a solution, three things are possible: (1) you haven't correctly identified your *real* interests; (2) there's an option you haven't thought of that will satisfy both of your interests, or (3) there are no viable options and you have a genuine difference of opinion that can't be resolved. It happens, but not as often as people think it happens. If you can eliminate the first two possibilities, you either compromise or get some help or drop all or part of your tailoring and just do the basic agreement. Help resources are discussed in the next section.

B.   Decide if you want help

If you are just doing the basic Couples Contract (chapter 2), there are only positive and useful things in there—not much to challenge you. But if you're digging deeper and thinking about financial or faith-based tailoring, you might come to a point where it would be good to find someone to talk to who can act as a sounding board, help you organize your facts and thoughts, give feedback, another point of view, suggest options you might not have thought of. Read through this book first, discuss it together, and write down any areas that you think need clarification or where you'd like some outside advice.

Who can help. It would be best to get help from someone who is familiar with this book or at least willing to read it (without charge). At least ask about this possibility. For some kinds of questions, you could talk things over with a mentor, wise friend, clergy, or couples counselor. An accountant could help you clarify your financial picture, as could a financial planner. If your discussions become difficult or heated, a good mediator can be invaluable to help you bore down to interests and explore options you haven't thought about. For overall review and help with suggestions and finding options to achieve your goals, nothing beats a good family law attorney with training and experience in making agreements designed to last. Unfortunately, most lawyers don't have these skills, which is why we recommend family law attorneys who specialize in mediation as their primary form of practice. A mediator's attitude is less adversarial and more oriented toward looking for solutions that satisfy both sides to any discussion.

Representation, advice, review. Most attorneys want to represent you, which means negotiating and drafting your agreement. But this can be very expensive, especially as they will want you to each have a separate attorney, and you really don't want to be represented anyway, unless absolutely necessary for reasons we explain below. But just getting some advice is much more affordable and a family law attorney who specializes in mediation would be an ideal person to go to for information, advice and options when it comes to tailoring financial relationships.

If you want to make sure your agreement is in good form, it would be ideal if you could have an attorney review it before you sign. However, finding the right attorney to help you can be its own kind of problem.

The problem. An attorney is typically concerned with two things: (1) planning for everything that might go wrong, and (2) how to get the greatest advantage for the one person he/she represents. The Couples Contract represents the common good of the relationship, whereas an attorney is legally obligated to pursue the best interests of one party. We believe that most couples would rather avoid negative thinking and arm's-length dealing and put their energy into a more constructive vision of their future. The agreement you are trying to create is a new and different thing. It is intensely personal and comes primarily from your heart at a time when you are looking forward to a long life together, which is why you might not want an attorney's heavy hand on it. Most attorneys won't ever have seen a Couples Contract and, if you do show it to them, some might want to tear it to pieces—not because there's anything actually wrong, but because it's not the way they're used to doing things or because attacking it is one way of proving that you need their services.

Many professionals distrust things that are different, and the Couples Contract is *very* different. It proceeds from positive and constructive principles; it has ideals and goals that are foreign to traditional marital agreements; it uses non-legalistic loving language; it includes clauses designed to help you solve relationship issues that are not enforceable in court; and, we instruct you to go through steps and procedures that attorneys have never used because they make your agreement enforceable without anyone being represented by an attorney.

Possible solutions. If you want to talk to a family law attorney, call for an appointment but first verify that the attorney specializes in family law mediation and does little or no litigation. When you show up for your appointment, tell the attorney that you (the couple) are thinking about making an agreement about your financial affairs and you want some suggestions and advice but do not want to be represented in the process. Next, ask if they are familiar with Nolo's Couples Contract and have read this book or if they are willing to read it on their own time to become familiar with it. If not, or if you don't want to have this discussion, you could simply work on the financial features separately and not distract the attorney with the rest of your agreement. Shop around before you settle on one and verify the charge for meeting to talk about possible services before you go in. Ideally, you would want an attorney who has read this book and seems enthusiastic and in tune with the concepts in it.

C.   How to assemble your extended agreement

Notice that we said *assemble* rather than *draft* or *write*. We've already done most of the drafting for you, so most couples will be able to put an agreement together from clauses found in this book and on the companion CD. So first we'll tell you how to assemble your agreement, then we'll explain how to modify clauses or draft new clauses that are different from the ones we prepared for you.

1.   Assembling your agreement

To assemble your agreement, simply get the clauses you want to use from the companion CD. Appendix D discusses how to use the CD and the files on it. If you don't have a computer and can't borrow or rent one, you can type the clauses directly from the book. While not common or even desirable, handwritten documents are just as legal as typed ones if they are neat and legible.

a.   Do the basic. Start with the basic agreement, following the instructions in chapter 2, using the typewriter or computer method. If you are only doing the basic agreement, skip to chapter 8 (checklist step 7).

b.   Add variations, if any. The basic agreement is the structure for your entire agreement. If you add any of the variations described in chapters 5–7, simply insert the clauses you choose, or others that you have decided to write yourselves, into the basic agreement, as instructed in those chapters. Be sure to keep the section and paragraph numbers in order if you change or add clauses or data.

If you are tailoring financial relationships, prepare the disclosure statements (chapter 5F) and attach them to your agreement as Schedules 1 and 2.

Decide if you want advice or help with adding variations (section B above).

c.   Make drafts until final. Make a draft of your agreement and go over it together. Make any agreed changes and go over it again. Repeat until you both think it is final.

d.   Review? If you decide to have an attorney review your agreement before you sign, now is the time to do it (section B above).

   e.   **Final agreement.** When you have both examined the draft agreement and approved it, make two duplicate originals of your final agreement, one for each of you. Go on to step 7 in the checklist.

2.   How to write clauses

Our recommended language is not cast in stone, but it has been carefully thought through by family law attorneys. In the text that runs alongside the template, we point out clauses where you can feel more free to write your own language, otherwise we suggest you be cautious about doing so. If you *do* decide to write your own clauses or modify ours, you must be precise and clear with your wording and also make sure you've covered all aspects of your subject. For example, if you state that certain property is the separate property of one person, you also have to say what happens to income from it, or appreciation, or what happens if marital funds are used to pay for or improve it, and what happens to debts that are incurred for the benefit of the separate property. If it's not complete, you'll end up with holes in your understanding or things that haven't been defined clearly.

   Use simple, plain language that cannot possibly be interpreted to mean more than one thing. Be careful with punctuation, as that can sometimes change meaning. Whatever you put in your agreement must be so clear that anyone can understand exactly what you mean. One way to check on this is to show your clauses to a friend and see if he/she can understand it from reading it (*not* by you explaining it verbally). Don't just say, "Do you understand it?" Have your friend repeat back to you in their own words what they think you are agreeing to do. If it is not exactly right, change your wording and try it on a different friend. If you write your own clauses, or modify ours, even if your friends get it perfectly, it would be a very good idea to have an attorney review your agreement. See section B above.

3.   Make it nice

Give some thought to making your Couples Contract look special. After all, this is a momentous special occasion. Use high-quality paper, parchment or vellum, and consider using a nice font. If you don't find a font you like on your computer, search the Internet for "free fonts." It is generally best to use just one nice font for the entire document, and you should avoid fonts that are not easy to read. Put your agreement in a handsome folder or binder, maybe add some photos of the signing, and you'll have something worthy of your relationship. To reduce clutter and preserve privacy in case you want to show your agreement off to someone, you might want to put all attachments—the Nolo Rules and any financial disclosures—in a sealed envelope marked "Attachments" that is inserted immediately after your Couples Contract. Similarly, you could also put related legal documents, such as the waivers and explanations, in a different sealed envelope that is kept behind your lovely Couples Contract and photos.

CHAPTER

4

How the law governs your relationship and when it matters

Before financial tailoring

"Tailoring" means to change your legal relationships by written agreement from what is provided by law, to better suit your particular circumstances or preferences. But, in order to think about tailoring your financial relationships (chapter 5), you first need to know what the existing rules are in your home state so you can decide how well they suit you as they stand. One of the purposes of this chapter is to help you do this.

* * *

In our family law practices, one of the most common things we hear over and over from clients who have just had the law explained to them is, "I wish I had known that a long time ago!" Or, "If only I had known that before (whatever) happened."

People entering any form of long-term relationship, whether married or just living together, are typically unaware that their relationship to each other—and to third parties, like creditors or government agencies—are defined and governed by rules of law, often in ways they did not expect or would not have agreed to had they known. They are not aware of what can happen when events force these rules into play.

Another surprise is that new laws can come along at any time and change your legal relationship in significant ways without you knowing or agreeing to it. And that's nothing compared to what can happen when you move to another state. Rights and duties that you might or might not have been aware of will suddenly become entirely different. Law books are filled with the cases of unhappy people who found out after the fact that things were not as they had thought or wished.

It is much better if you do not wait in ignorance for some defining event to spring up and force the rules to your attention. We encourage every couple to know where they stand and learn how and to what extent they can tailor their legal relationship to more closely suit their personal wishes.

A. Your legal relationships have already been defined

If you are in a long-term relationship and do not have an *enforceable* written agreement, rules of law define and govern important features of your relationship—such things as:

- How open and honest you must be with each other about finances
- Who owns income earned by either of you during the relationship
- Who can manage the money and assets
- Who owes debts incurred by either of you before or during the relationship
- Who owns property acquired during the relationship
- Who can parent children or adopt
- Who can be covered by health insurance
- Who can get family care leave
- Who can authorize medical or mental health treatment
- Who can visit in a hospital or jail
- Who can order care and apply for benefits after disability
- Who inherits if there is no will
- Who is included in the retirement plan
- Who sees to the partner's wishes after death

You have a choice: accept the rules imposed by law, or tailor the terms of your relationship in a written agreement to better suit your needs and preferences.

B. When the rules matter—events that force the issue

You might go for years without encountering an event that forces your legal relationships to your attention, or something might happen tomorrow, or you might wander into a situation and not realize the consequences until it's too late.

If you don't know the rules (and who amongst us knows them all?), you can at least be aware that there *are* rules, where to find them, and—most important—when you need to know how they work.

Below is a list of events that might bring the rules into play and to your attention. Some events are more relevant to married couples, some to unmarried couples, but they are all of interest. Section C discusses how rules of law are applied, and sections D and E discuss how rules can change without you being told about it. Section F is a list of our suggestions for things every couple should do.

Example events that can bring the rules into play

Filing income tax returns	Deciding to have or adopt a child
Large debts or a risky business	Applying for financial aid for a child
Seeking health insurance	
Purchasing on credit	Moving to another state
Borrowing money	Saving for retirement
Refinancing your home	Retirement
Immigration issues	Loss of job or income
Buying or renting a place to live	Applying for benefits
Transfer of real estate to the other	Accident
Making gifts to your mate or others	Chronic illness
	Death or disability
Naming someone else as insurance or pension beneficiary	Bankruptcy
	Getting sued
Applying for Social Security	Acts of discrimination
	Splitting up

C. How the rules are applied

If an event comes up that puts the rules into play and the matter were to end up in front of a judge, the judge would look first to see if you have an *enforceable* agreement that applies. An agreement is not enforceable unless it meets an array of legal requirements, but don't worry—if you follow the steps in this book, your Couples Contract will be enforceable. If you have an enforceable agreement, its terms will be followed. If not, the matter will be decided according to the rules of law for people in your form of relationship: marriage, civil union, or unmarried and living together. But remember: if you have a Couples Contract, you are unlikely to ever come before a judge in any event.

D. Volatility—when rules change

Marriage has been an established institution for many centuries, yet lawmakers continue to tinker with the rights and duties of married people. Significant changes might take place only from time to time, but you never know when this can happen and no one sends you a notice, like credit card companies must do, telling you that your contract has just been changed by forces beyond your control. This is one good reason for making written agreements, so your legal relationship stays put.

Civil union and same-sex marriage are the Wild, Wild West of relationship law. Same-sex couples are battling mightily against stiff opposition for equal rights and legal recognition. California and Vermont recognize same-sex unions, but not marriages. In 2005, Canada became the third country, after the Netherlands and Belgium, to recognize same-sex marriage, so we now have U.S. gay couples with valid Canadian marriage licenses, calling into question the obligation of U.S. states under international treaties at a time when at least 18 states have enacted constitutional amendments banning them. Massachusetts lawmakers voted down a change to the state constitution that would ban gay marriage, which leaves in effect, for now, the Massachusetts Supreme Court ruling that legislation prohibiting same-sex marriage violates the state constitution. Meanwhile, a federal judge ruled that the same-sex marriage ban in Nebraska's constitution violates the U.S. Constitution. What a shambles! The rules governing same-sex relationships will be fought over and continue to be unstable for years to come. If this is your area of interest, you should watch special-interest Web sites, such as www.lambdalegal.org.

E. Couples on the move

The laws of the state where you reside are what define your legal relationships, and this almost guarantees that significant changes will occur when you move from one state to another. For example, in California, the earned income of either spouse is community property that belongs to both and both have the right to spend it or sell property purchased with it. However, in many states, income belongs to the spouse who earned it, as does anything purchased with that income. This is quite a big difference, determined solely by where you reside.

With a Couples Contract, you are mostly freed from this concern when you agree that the laws of your home state will govern all matters in your relationship, wherever you might move. This will prevent surprises in your financial affairs, but child custody and support will always come under the laws of whatever state a child lives in, no matter what your agreement says.

Another possible option is to agree that you will only be bound by laws in existence at the time you sign your contract, but this is a two-edged sword: yes, you avoid surprises, but if a new law comes along that could have improved your lot in life, you'll miss out. It also means you need to review the laws periodically to see if you want to get on board with anything new.

If you move to another state after you make a Couples Contract, you need to review the laws of your new state before you make the move, or as soon as possible afterward. Some of your rights and obligations as a couple will probably have changed in significant ways that you should know about. If you have a written agreement, you also want to know how your new state interprets agreements made by a couple in another state.

F. Learning about couples law in your state

Forms of ownership

In the Couples Contract, we use "marital property" and refer to the "marital estate" to describe assets the parties intend to own together, but this is not a form of ownership that might appear on a deed or title document. In fact, property can be deemed by a court to be a marital asset regardless of how title is specified in the deed. So, "marital property" is a legal conclusion, not a form of ownership.

When owning property together, any couple can take title as either joint tenants or tenants in common. Married couples have the additional option of taking title as community property in states that have that form of ownership, or as tenants in the entirety in other states.

The right of survivorship—meaning that when one co-owner dies the surviving owner automatically owns the deceased person's share—is an inherent feature of joint tenancy and tenancy by the entirety, but not community property. However, Arizona, California, Nevada, Texas, and Wisconsin offer the optional "community property with right of survivorship" that does include it.

The title to property might not be conclusive as to actual ownership. For example, a Couples Contract can specify that upon marriage, a house owned separately by the wife will become marital property, even though the deed continues to show the wife as sole owner. Or, if a couple uses marital funds to buy a house during marriage, the house is marital property, even if title is taken solely in the name of the husband.

In your Couples Contract, you can specify that certain items of property are or will become separate or marital property and you can also agree to execute a new instrument (such as a deed) changing the form of title. You must be very careful that you fully understand the meaning of each form of ownership, otherwise you might get unintended results. For example, if you co-own property as joint tenants, tenants by the entirety, or community property with right of survivorship, you can only own it in equal shares and cannot leave your share to others in a will because of the right of survivorship. By contrast, people who co-own property as tenants in common can take ownership in unequal shares and each can sell his/her share or leave it to others in a will.

If you plan to tailor your Couples Contract so that you will own property other than as separate property or marital property, consult an attorney in your state to make sure you're getting the results you want and none that you don't want.

If you intend to change ownership in property from one form of ownership to another, this is called "transmutation"—for example, changing the ownership of a house from one spouse's separate property to marital property or to the separate property of the other spouse. Many states have strict rules about how transmutation can take place that must be followed or the transmutation might fail, so if you intend to do this, you should get some advice from an attorney in your state.

Management and control of income and assets

In all states, each spouse has sole management and control of his/her own separate property. As to marital assets, all states hold that one spouse may never act in fraud of the other's rights. In most states, the husband has the management and control of marital assets, subject to a fiduciary duty to act prudently and make full disclosures to his wife. Many other states, including most of those that have adopted the community-property system[1], give spouses equal management and control of marital (community) property, and some require the signatures of both spouses to convey community real estate, even if only one spouse's name is on the title. In practical terms, rules about who controls jointly owned assets lose significance whenever both signatures are required to convey or encumber the asset, as could be the case for such things as real estate, vehicles, and bank or investment accounts. Because states vary on this, you'll want to find out how management and control of property works in your home state (see 4G below).

---

[1] The community property states are Arizona, California, Idaho, Louisiana, Nevada, New Mexico, Texas, Washington, and Wisconsin, plus Puerto Rico. Spouses in Alaska can elect CP ownership.

Rights of surviving spouses

Most states have some form of protection for surviving spouses, giving them an interest in their deceased spouse's estate. A few states award a life-estate in some portion of the decedent's estate, while others award a choice of either taking whatever was given under the decedent's will or electing instead to take a specific fraction of the decedent's estate. The fraction is typically one-third or one-half, depending on the state. In some situations—say, people getting married near or after retirement and otherwise well-provided for—spouses making a Couples Contract might want to give up (waive) any right they might have in the estate of the other spouse (see chapter 5D(3)).

Read more. An article about inheritance and the rights of a surviving spouse appears in the Legal Briefs folder on the companion CD.

What creditors can take

When you don't pay a debt, the creditor can get a judgment and go after your income and assets, but states vary as to what they can take, so you'll want to look into the rules for your home state. An article on this subject appears in the Legal Briefs folder on the companion CD.

More things you might want to know

This list is meant to suggest ways the laws in your state might affect your own financial situation, but it is not necessarily exhaustive. After you read chapter 5 about financial tailoring, you might come up with other questions to ask, then you can go about getting some answers as suggested in section G below.

Married couples

Assets and debts before union

Under what circumstances can the marital estate acquire an interest in separate property of a spouse?

What becomes of income and appreciation from separate assets?

Finances during union

What duty does one spouse owe the other in their financial dealings?

Who has the right to control income and assets?

Can either party alone make gifts of jointly owned assets?

Who owns assets acquired during the marriage?

Who owns gifts or inherited assets?

Who owns a gift given by one spouse to the other?

How does the way title to property is held affect actual ownership?

What happens if jointly owned income or assets are used to benefit the separate property of one spouse?

Can a joint interest be acquired in a spouse's separate property?

What happens when you mix joint and separate property (e.g., putting separate income in a joint account)?

What are the rules for how you change (transmute) property from one form of ownership to another (e.g., from separate to marital, or vice-versa)?

How will joint expenses be paid?

Who is responsible for joint debts?

Can joint or separate assets of one be reached by creditors to pay for a debt of the other?

Must changes in character (i.e., separate or joint) of assets be made in writing?

What if marital funds are used to benefit one spouse's child from a previous relationship?

At the end

What are your rights if one of you dies?

How is property divided on divorce?

What is the duty to support a spouse or child?

Unmarried couples

Does your state have common-law marriage? If so, how does one end up married under that law?

Do unmarried people who cohabit have any duty higher than that of strangers when dealing with one another?

Under what circumstances (if any) do unmarried people acquire a duty to support one another? That is, does your state recognize "palimony"?

Are there any laws that govern or protect people in unmarried relationships? (Probably not, and that's the problem in a nutshell: no rights, no definitions. You have to create any rights you want to have with contracts, wills, trusts, titles, and other documents.)

Medical

Can you visit your loved one in the hospital?

Can you order care for an incapacitated loved one?

Is one entitled to health insurance through the employment of the other?

G. How to get some answers

1. Get advice

Perhaps the best thing you can do, and certainly the easiest, would be to pay for an hour or so with a family law attorney in your home state. See chapter 3B for tips on how to choose an attorney. To make sure you use the time efficiently, prepare for your meeting a long time ahead:

- Read this book.
- Write down all the questions you want answered.
- Write down the facts and circumstances of your life that are relevant to your questions.
  - State whether you are currently married, or plan to marry, and give the date in either case.
  - For each of you, list age, residence, state of health, education, occupation.
  - State whether or not there are children of your relationship and, if so, their names and ages. Similarly, indicate if there are children by either of you from a prior or other relationship and, if so, list their names and ages.
  - Mention any significant future plans or anticipated events that might be relevant, such as a move or an anticipated inheritance.
  - Complete the disclosure worksheet on the CD in the chapter 5 folder.
- Make copies of the information and take them to your appointment. In the office, ask questions about how laws in your state affect couples in your situation. Also ask if the attorney can suggest where you can find answers on your own. He/she will know where the law books and practice guides are kept and which are most useful.

2. Books in print

There might be books written for the public that discuss marriage and family laws for your state. Go to your local public library and ask the reference librarian or look in their catalog for listings under topics such as marital property, family law, premarital or prenuptial agreements, marital agreements, cohabitation, marriage law, and so on. Look in *Books in Print* in the reference section under similar topics. A good book store should also have a copy of *Books in Print* that they will probably let you browse.

3. Law library

Most states have books for attorneys that describe and discuss family law in your state. Look for a law library that is open to the public—ask a lawyer or call the courthouse. When you go there, ask the law librarian how to find general information about family laws in your state.

4. On-line research

Go to www.nolo.com/statute where you will find links to lookup pages for state or federal statutes with tips on statute research.

Go to www.findlaw.com for maybe too much legal information. Browse around. Among other things, under the column "For Legal Professionals," click on "Cases & Codes," or "States."

H. Things every couple should do

1. Be aware of the rules and when they matter

Having read this chapter, you now know that a vast body of cases and statutes govern your marital, financial, and parenting relationships, as well as your relationships with third parties, like creditors, government agencies, retirement plans, and so on. Ideally, you will learn at least in general about how these laws affect you and your relationship. Use the questions in sections A and F that seem to be about you, and the methods in section G to get some answers.

2. Make a Couples Contract

You should definitely do the basic Couples Contract described in chapter 2. Every couple should. It doesn't matter if you are married, getting married, or unmarried and living together: if you are a committed couple, you want this agreement.

3. Think, discuss and plan together

The Couples Contract is something you will want to do together. This doesn't mean that one of you can't spend a few hours to prepare the paperwork, but both of you should take some time to discuss the ideas and options in the basic agreement and consider whether you want to do financial tailoring or add faith-based features at this time, later or never. Chapter 3 has a checklist for how to proceed and some advice about how to work together on additions to your basic agreement.

4. Who can help?

The basic Couples Contract is relatively simple and uncompli-cated, so it will be no surprise if you do yours without any help at all beyond this book.

There are a few places in the chapters on financial and faith-based tailoring where we suggest that some people might want to get information and advice from an accountant, financial planner, estate planner, clergy or family law attorney, depending on the subject being discussed. If you add financial tailoring or otherwise depart from our template, it could be very useful to have your agreement reviewed by a family law attorney before you make the final draft. Read chapter 3B for a discussion about finding the right kind of help.

CHAPTER

5

Variations to tailor your financial relationships

This chapter is primarily for people who are married,[1] or who plan to marry. Unmarried couples who do not plan to marry should first skip to chapter 7, then return here to browse for ideas, then on through the checklist.

A. Who should do it

First, let's find out if you are one of those couples who should do financial tailoring. Remember, you can always do the basic Couples Contract first and add financial features later. **Unmarried?** Unmarried couples who are not planning to get married *definitely* need to make some financial agreements. Definitely! Read chapter 7 right now.

Is off-the-shelf OK? If you don't add tailoring to your basic agreement, your financial and parenting affairs are governed by the laws of your home state, one size fits all. Most couples live under whatever rules their state provides, never giving them much thought and, if they move to other state, not giving the new rules much thought either. But state law is not equally suitable for everyone. A lot of couples, even of quite modest means, can improve their situations by tailoring their financial relationships. Tailoring can, for example, make special arrangements for such things as:

- Reducing tension caused when one spouse
  is far more thrifty than the other or in a risky business
- Children of a prior relationship
- A separate business or professional practice
- A couple getting married near or during retirement
- Personal preferences that are different from state law

Get information, consider, discuss. You can't do tailoring to change your relationship from what state law provides unless you know what state law provides. Read chapter 4G and use any of the methods described there to find out how the laws in your state affect you. Review sections C and D below to see if any of the examples remind you of circumstances in your life that might benefit from

---

[1] Applies also to same-sex couples in those few states that provide for substantially equal rights and duties for same-sex couples who register a Civil Union or Domestic Partnership.

financial tailoring. Discuss financial tailoring with your spouse or partner, talk about what you might like to accomplish, and decide if you want to do it.

B. The romantic side of money discussions

If you think you might benefit from tailoring your financial relationships, you will have to have some detailed discussions with your significant other about money and property. For those who are still in the throes of romance and love, this might seem like a burden on your bliss: a dash of cold water when all you desire is to keep those fires burning. Even if you've been living together for years, discussing financial affairs can seem as appealing as having your teeth drilled.

If you can't discuss money . . . well, don't you have to wonder how strong your relationship is? You're not alone if just thinking about it makes you nervous. Most couples don't handle money discussions very well. In fact, failure to come to terms with money is a leading cause of breakups, even ahead of infidelity. Many experts believe that marital agreements can actually strengthen relationships, because by dealing with money matters you can either expose a problem area that needs attention or eliminate it as a possible threat to your future. Financial discussions will give you the valuable experience of working together on a demanding task and help build a sound foundation for your future.

Disclosure. If you're going to do financial tailoring, you *must* exchange financial information in writing so that you both have the opportunity to make decisions based on full awareness of the facts. This is called *disclosure*. In fact, we recommend disclosure in every case, whether required or not, as full exchange of information and discussion of financial matters builds trust and a solid foundation for any couple's future. How to do disclosure is described in section F below.

Advice. Be sure to read chapter 3A, which has tips that will help you work together more smoothly. Go over each other's financial information together, as described in section F below. Consider going to a certified financial planner or family law attorney for advice (chapter 3B). Discuss your goals, our sample agreement clauses, and ideas for what could go in your own agreement. Agree on specific clauses to use.

C. What an agreement can (and can't) do

Tailoring can define your relationship to premarital assets and debts of either one of you, and to your marital finances: assets, income, expenses, debts, parenting, support and estate matters. In each category, you have options for how your relationship to them can be modified, as outlined below. The next section shows how these options can be applied to tailor representative situations commonly faced by couples. It doesn't matter whether you read section C or D first, as you'll probably end up going back and forth once you begin to see how tailoring can apply (or not) to your own situation.

The things you can do

Here is the range of things financial tailoring can accomplish in your Couples Contract. In this discussion, we use "marital estate" for things the spouses own together, but some states use different terms, like "community" or "joint," and so on. You should find out the terms of property ownership used in your home state and use them in your Couples Contract (more about terminology in chapter 4F).

1. Define premarital assets and debts

Clarify how you will treat assets owned and debts owed by each of you prior to marriage—real estate, a business or professional practice, retirement plans, savings or investment accounts, and specific special possessions. Even if you are making your agreement after marriage, it is still possible to agree on the status and treatment of assets and debts that were owned before marriage. These are the issues; see if any of them might apply to you:

- Will separate assets and debts continue to be separate after marriage?
- What happens if you use marital funds to pay off a separate debt, pay the mortgage on separate real estate, or improve a separate property?
- What happens if a separate asset appreciates or is sold?

a. Assets
Your agreement can treat all items the same, or various items differently, by agreeing that on marriage, one or all or your existing assets:

- Will become marital property.
- Will be apportioned between marital and separate property according to a list or formula.

- Will remain separate and
  - * All traceable profits or increases remain separate.
  - * Marital estate acquires an interest to extent it pays down the mortgage or makes improvements that increase value.
  - * Marital estate acquires no interest under any circumstances.
  - * Marital estate acquires no interest, but
    - – Marital estate contributions to be reimbursed (with interest?).
    - – Profits or increases in value will be marital property.

b. Debts

Your agreement can't prevent creditors from reaching marital assets to pay the premarital debts of either party, but spouses can arrange to have no marital assets (i.e., have all property owned as separate property) and they can agree between themselves who will be responsible for certain debts and what will happen between them if marital assets are used to pay them.

- Each to be responsible for his/her own premarital and/or marital debts.
- If marital assets are used or taken to pay separate debts, the marital estate is entitled to reimbursement (plus x% interest).
- The marital estate will pay off all debts with no reimbursement.

2. Define marital finances

Clarify how you will handle income, expenses, debts, and assets acquired during marriage, including such things as real estate, businesses or professional practices, inheritances, gifts, retirement benefits, and so on. Your agreement can treat all items the same, or various items differently, by agreeing how to treat one or more items in each category:

a. Income

- Earned income will be marital property.
- Earned income will be the separate property of the recipient.
- Earned income will be apportioned according to a formula.

b. Marital expenses

- Owed by the marital estate.
- Shared according to some plan or formula.
- To be paid by one person.

c. Debts incurred during marriage

Your agreement can't change the rights of creditors created by the law or by contracts you make with them, but spouses can agree between themselves who will be responsible for certain debts and what will happen between them if marital or separate assets are used to pay them.

- The marital estate will be responsible for certain debts. If separate funds are used, the marital estate will reimburse the spouse who pays them.
- Each responsible for own debts incurred during marriage and marital funds will be reimbursed (plus x% interest) if marital funds used to pay such debts.
- Treat differently debts incurred for mutual benefit vs. debts incurred by a spouse in operation of a separate business.

d. Assets acquired during marriage

- Marital property if acquired with marital funds.
- Gifts or inheritances to just one spouse will be separate property.
- Assets to be kept entirely separate, no marital rights accrue.
- Determined according to how title is held.
- Owned proportionately according to a formula.

3. Children

Your agreement can provide for the care of your children or children of a previous relationship (stepchildren). We recommend that you do not make commitments to support children through advanced education; there are so many variables that to make a specific agreement far in advance is unwise. For example, the child could sue if you declined to fund her halfhearted attendance in some program that you did not care to support. This matter is best dealt with when the time comes.

4. Future plans

This includes such things as treatment of anticipated inheritances, saving for children's college education, buying a house, and so on.

5. In case of separation

You can define what will happen in case one or both of you want to separate or divorce. We feel this is handled well enough for most couples by the mediation/arbitration provision and the financial tailoring clauses, but if you have a family business or particular assets you want to protect, you'll probably want to consult a family law attorney for more options (see chapter 3B).

6. Estate matters

We do not cover the subject of wills and estate planning in this book because the subject is huge and because we do not believe that the terms of such plans should normally be included in a Couples Contract. However, in certain situations, as where retired people, each with their own sufficient estates, decide to marry but want to leave most of their estates to their own heirs, it might be appropriate for each to waive all inheritance rights and claims against the estate of the other, or variations on that theme. If you want estate planning terms in your agreement, we suggest you call a certified estate planner, a certified financial planner, or an attorney who specializes in estate planning for advice and assistance.

Read more. An article about inheritance and the rights of surviving spouses appears in the Legal Briefs folder on the companion CD.

Considered part of estate planning, everyone should have a Health Care Directive, a very important document that is so easy, you can do it yourself (see section G below).

Limitations—things you can't do

Most limitations on relationship agreements are understandable, like not being allowed to agree to a criminal act or make an agreement that would defraud creditors; say, by putting all marital property in one person's name just before the other is about to be sued. A bit less clear is the rule that you can't make an agreement that goes against public policy—for example, rewarding someone for getting a divorce or trying to limit the courts' authority to protect the best interests of children. But, don't worry; if you stay close to our model, you'll stay clear of legal limitations.

1. Creditors[2]

Sometimes one spouse needs protection from past debts, or potential future debts, of the other. The rules of state law can be redefined between spouses by agreement, but no matter what you agree between yourselves about how debts will be paid, creditors who *already* have a right against your separate or marital assets will not be affected. Your agreement can only affect new creditors who know, or had the opportunity to know, that you keep your income separate and have disavowed responsibility for each other's debts. To protect your income and separate assets, you must take practical steps:

- Make a Couples Contract that defines all income, assets and debts as separate (section D below)
- Keep your earnings in an account in your own name that your spouse cannot access
- Cancel all joint accounts and credit cards, then get new ones in your name only
- Never co-sign with your spouse on any accounts or credit applications that you don't want to be liable for
- Have any agreement on this point reviewed by a family law attorney to see if it is sufficient under your state's laws (see chapter 3B).

2. Out-of-state property

Arbitrators and judges can make decisions about out-of-state property, but cannot directly change title to property in another state. If you own property in some other state or country, you have to inquire there to find out how they go about enforcing an arbitrator's award or a court judgment from the state where your case was concluded. It'll probably work out fine, but you won't know how or for sure until you do the research or get legal advice in the jurisdiction where the property is located.

---

[2] An article about what creditors can take and from whom appears in the Legal Briefs folder on the companion CD.

3. Child and spousal support

Be cautious about spousal support. Some states are hypersensitive about spousal support. It would seem they want to protect women (or any spouses) who sign agreements from an unequal bargaining position, but for sure they want to make sure nobody ends up living at public expense after a breakup. We can't think of very many good reasons for tinkering with spousal support, but if this is something you feel strongly about, you should get advice from a family law attorney in your state to discuss how you must go about doing it.

Don't touch child support. The right to support belongs to the child and is zealously guarded by courts who will not give up their authority over it, so don't attempt to limit child support without advice from a family law attorney as to what can be done in your state and how to do it.

D. Example situations with sample clauses

Our goal here is to illustrate some reasonable solutions for situations encountered by some couples across the economic spectrum. For a broader range of possibilities, take a look at Nolo's excellent book, *Prenuptial Agreements,* by Stoner and Irving. You can find large volumes in law libraries (chapter 4G) that are full of variations and possibilities for premarital and marital contracts, but we can't cover them all here.

After wrangling with ourselves over these examples, we came to realize that a slight change in circumstances might require different terms and most examples could become complicated if we kept asking, "What if?" We've come to believe that unless your situation is clear and the financial clauses obvious, you would be better served to do your homework here then talk it over with an experienced family law attorney (chapter 3B) to get some ideas and options or to review a draft of your Couples Contract.

Common situations. The situations illustrated below are common to many couples, organized according to their primary factual concern, as follows:

Sample clauses. For each example situation, we show sample clauses that could be used to tailor the couple's financial relationships by adding them to their basic Couples Contract. We describe in detail how to add financial clauses in section E below.

Explanations. After each sample clause we also show a sample explanation that you can use in the Explanation of Agreement document, which is discussed in chapter 8A.

Read them all. Many of the sample solutions use a variety of options, so you should read the agreements used in every example, as some clause used for a seemingly unrelated situation might trigger a thought about your own life.

Get help. These examples and solutions are relatively simple. Unless your situation and tailoring efforts are also simple and straightforward, we urge you to have a family law attorney review financial and parenting terms of your agreement (see chapter 3B).

1. Clarifying the treatment of separate property

Lots of people have separate property when they get married that is either of special meaning or value or both. Not everyone wants to mix their separate property into the marital estate, but in some states, the marital estate can get an interest in it over time, even without anyone intending it—unless there's an agreement, that is. In situations like the three examples below, it is much better if you write down what you intend to have happen to your separate property. If you're already married, you can still clarify what is separate and what is not.

a. Situation

K was in a marriage that ended badly. She struggled for years and was finally able to buy her own home. K has just married L, a gardener who might go back to school to study art history. For her own sense of security, she wants to keep the house separate and does not want the marital estate to acquire any interest in it.

Comment

In some states, the marital estate can acquire an interest in separate property to the extent that the mortgage is reduced by payments from marital funds, or the value is increased either by the effort of either spouse or by improvements paid for with funds earned by either spouse during marriage. To be safe in any state, you have to specify exactly how you want things to work.

b. Situation

B owns a condo and D owns a few acres in the country, about equal in value. They plan to sell the condo some day, buy a nice house they'll own together and eventually build a cottage on the country property. They agree that both separate properties will become marital property.

Comment

Changing the form of ownership is called "transmutation." We have you use the technical term in the contract because some states are strict and require absolute clarity of your intention. Note that the parties also agree to execute and record new deeds to reflect the new ownership. So, in Situation b, after marriage B would sign and record a deed conveying the condo "from B, as his separate property, to B and D, husband and wife, as [e.g., joint tenants/tenants in common/ tenants in the entirety/community property]." Likewise D would execute and record a deed conveying the country acreage from D to B and D.

Agreement for situation 1(a)

B.   K's house located at (address) is and will remain K's separate property, as will all rents and appreciation. Under no circumstances will the marital estate acquire an interest in K's house.

So long as we occupy K's house, the marital estate will not be reimbursed for marital funds used to pay the mortgage principal or interest, property taxes, insurance, maintenance, or repairs.

If we do not occupy K's house, the marital estate will be reimbursed for marital funds used to pay the mortgage, property taxes, insurance, maintenance, or repairs.

If marital funds are used at any time to pay for capital improvements to K's house, those funds will be reimbursed (Optional: plus __% interest per year) in the event that K dies, the house is sold, or we separate.

Explanation (for use in chapter 8A)

By signing this agreement, we agree that K's house at (address) is and will remain her separate property and that all rents and appreciation from it will also be her separate property. L is giving up the right to claim any interest in K's house under any circumstances. While we live in K's house, we may use marital funds to pay the mortgage, taxes, insurance, maintenance and repairs. L gives up the right to claim that these make the house partly marital property or to claim any reimbursement for these marital funds. If we don't live there, K will be completely responsible for all expenses connected with the house, and if marital funds are used in connection with the house while we don't live there, K will reimburse the marital estate. If the house is sold or if we separate or if K dies, the marital estate will also be reimbursed (with __% interest per year) for any marital funds spent on capital improvements, whether made while we live there or not.

Agreement for situation 1(b)

B.   We agree that upon the effective date of this agreement, B's condominium at (address) and D's property at (address or other description) will both be transmuted to marital property. All other property owned by either of us on the date of our marriage will remain the separate property of the person who owns it. We agree to sign new deeds on or after this agreement becomes effective changing title to these properties to [e.g. joint tenancy/tenancy by the entirety/community property with right of survivorship].

Or

B.   We agree that all property of every kind owned at this time by either of us will be transmuted to our marital property on the date this agreement takes effect. To the degree that either of us might now have any separate right or interest in any property, we transmute that interest to marital property. This does not apply to the ownership of property that either of us might acquire in the future. We agree to sign new deeds on or after this agreement becomes effective changing title to these properties to marital property (optional: with right of survivorship).

c. Situation

A and M each have rental properties that they want to keep separate, but because they will work together to manage their properties, they feel that profits from their properties should be marital property.

Comment

A and M agree to "indemnify, defend and hold (the other) harmless" from debts incurred for the benefit of their separate property. This means that each must make sure the other suffers no cost, inconvenience or impairment of credit, so they must either pay the debt or undertake the full burden of any letter-writing, negotiations, legal actions—whatever it takes to resolve the claim.

2. Children of a prior relationship

Situation

T and A both have children by prior relationships who will often be in their home. Rather than keep detailed accounting records, they decide it makes more sense to share all household expenses equally, including reasonable expenses for their children, by depositing all marital earnings, plus separate earnings if necessary and on an equal or pro-rated basis, into a joint account. Any child support payments received will also be deposited to the joint account.

Comment

The duty to support a child of another relationship is a separate obligation. In some states and under some circumstances, marital funds used to pay for a spouse's separate child support obligation are entitled to reimbursement. You both might feel better if you specify how marital and separate funds will be used to benefit stepchildren and to what extent there will be reimbursement. Here, we illustrate just one possible arrangement; you'll want to detail your own solution in your agreement.

Explanation (for use in chapter 8A)

We each now own separate property (listed on Schedule 3). We understand that we each have the right to keep all our separate property separate. We wish for

☐ (describe specific property to become marital property)

☐ all of our respective separate real properties (listed in Schedule 3)

to become marital property from the date this agreement takes effect, and understand that this agreement will accomplish this, whether or not we actually sign and record the deeds we have promised to sign. We are each freely and voluntarily giving up the right to keep separate these separate properties.

Agreement for situation 1(c)

B. The separate property assets belonging to A, listed on Schedule 3, and the separate property assets of M, listed on Schedule 4, are and will remain their own separate properties, but all net profits flowing from those properties will be their marital property from the effective date of this agreement.

A will be responsible for all debts incurred in the operation of or for the benefit of A's separate properties that cannot be paid from income therefrom and will indemnify, defend and hold M harmless from any action to collect such debts from marital assets or M's separate property, including paying any costs and attorney fees in connection with such an action.

M will be responsible for all debts incurred in the operation of or for the benefit of M's separate properties that cannot be paid from income therefrom and will indemnify, defend and hold A harmless from any action to collect such debts from marital assets or A's separate property, including paying any costs and attorney fees in connection with such an action.

Explanation

We understand that our respective separate real properties, listed in Schedules 3 and 4, will remain separate, but that we are each giving up the right to keep separate ownership of net profits from our separate properties, choosing instead to make it marital property. We are agreeing to each be responsible for all debts incurred for the benefit of or in the operation of our separate properties that are in excess of profits realized from those properties.

Agreement for situation 2

B. T has children of a prior relationship: Terry, age 10 and Tommy, age 7. A has children of a prior relationship: Annie, age 6 and Andrew, age 3. We each love and welcome the other's children into our home as we would our own natural children. We agree that marital resources can be used for their benefit for all ordinary costs of living, health insurance, education, court-ordered child support and medical care. Each of us waives any right to reimbursement. All children will be named as beneficiaries of each of our health insurance policies, to the extent they are eligible, and will be named as beneficiaries in any wills or life insurance policies on an equal basis with our own natural or adopted children, if any. Any child support or other funds received for any child will be deposited into our joint accounts. If marital income is not sufficient to pay all marital expenses, we will make deposits from our separate funds on an equal basis into our joint account in amounts necessary to cover all expenses.

3. Marriage after retirement

Situation

L, age 67 and J, age 70, both have grown children from earlier relationships, adequate nest eggs, and small monthly incomes from consulting and freelance activities. They want to marry, but feel it doesn't suit them to embrace their state's family law system and they want all their assets to descend to their own heirs.

Comment

Seniors who are married or marrying sometimes have fears from past divorce trauma or their children could be concerned that their parent's estate might be drained away by the new spouse, or their inheritance lost or that financial or emotional advantage is being taken. The children of senior couples would not want a family feud after their parents pass on, so they might be more comfortable if both parties were represented by separate attorneys to make their agreement as bulletproof as possible. The more value in the estate, the stronger our recommendation that you secure independent counsel for both parties, if for no other reason than to reassure the children. With counsel, you will not need the Explanation document and the attorneys will assist in the negotiating, drafting and signing of your agreement. Show them this book and tell them that you want the positive and constructive features of it in your agreement, in addition to the financial ones that they will construct for you.

Clause G and a possible variation

As written, clause G is a complete and total waiver by both spouses of any right or interest in the separate estate of the other in the event of death, except where they have expressly been made a beneficiary of a will, trust, or insurance policy. You would only want to make this kind of waiver if both were well-provided for by their own estates or by other means. As an alternative, you could agree to leave the surviving spouse a life estate in the home, or a lease for a period of years at no rent. A life estate is the grant (by deed or will) of possession of property to a person (the "life tenant") for the lifetime of that person, or for the lifetime of another designated person. Upon the death of the designated person, possession automatically reverts to the grantor or his heirs.

Explanation

We agree to use marital resources for the benefit of our respective children by other relationships, and to include them as beneficiaries under any wills or health or life-insurance policies to the extent they are eligible. We understand that under some circumstances the marital estate can have a right to reimbursement of money paid as child support for children of other relationships, and that some payments for their education or life insurance for their benefit could be considered a gift, voidable by the other spouse or reimbursable to the marital estate. By this agreement, we are giving up all rights to claim reimbursement for such expenses or to treat money spent on the children as a gift made without the consent of the other spouse. We also agree to treat any child support that either of us may receive during our marriage as marital property and give up any right we may have to claim it as separate property.

Agreement for situation 3

B.   Separate assets. J's assets and debts, listed on Schedule 1, are and will continue to be J's separate property, along with all rents and appreciation, including profits resulting from the efforts of either of us. L's assets and debts, listed on Schedule 2, are and will continue to be L's separate property, along with all rents and appreciation, including profits resulting from the efforts of either of us. The marital estate will under no circumstances acquire any interest in J's or L's separate property.

We each consent to the other person naming whoever they wish as death beneficiary in their will, trust, retirement plan, account, insurance policy, or anything else that allows a person to designate a death beneficiary. We will each sign any documents required to carry out our intent.

C.   Marital assets and income to be separate. All property (real or personal) acquired during our marriage, including but not limited to income from personal services, pensions and retirement plans, and unearned income, will remain separate property of the spouse receiving it. J and L will maintain separate bank and credit accounts.

D.   Debts. J and L will be responsible for their own debts, whether incurred before or during the marriage, and each will indemnify, defend and hold harmless the other from any action to collect one's debts from the other's property, including paying any costs and attorney fees in connection with such an action.

E.   Expenses. J and L will, as necessary, make equal deposits into a joint bank account to pay for their joint living expenses, which they will share equally.

F.   Joint purchases. If J and L jointly purchase a home or other real estate, ownership will be according to the manner in which the title is held. Personal property will belong to the person who pays for it unless we make a separate writing to cover such property.

G.   Bequests. We each want our separate property to descend to our own heirs, therefore except as otherwise provided in this agreement, we each give up (waive, release, relinquish) any and all right, title or interest whatever, whether under common law or present or future statutes of any jurisdiction, in the separate property and probate estate of the other, including but not limited to community-property rights, the right to intestate distribution, the right of election or forced share against the will of the other, and any right to dower, curtesy, and statutory allowances. This waiver does not apply to

4. A party who is in debt, a spendthrift, or in a risky business

Situation

H owns a risky contracting business, likes to gamble, and is frequently in debt. S owns a separate home and has a steady, decent income that she wants to protect. They agree that it's safest for her if they keep everything separate.

Comments

In many states, the best way to prevent creditors of one spouse from reaching marital property is to arrange not to have marital property. You should check to see how this works in your state, as discussed in chapter 4G. When you follow this course, you need to follow through by carefully keeping everything truly separate because careless mixing of assets could undermine the plan. Don't open any joint accounts except the household checking account for routine expenses, and don't sign any loan or credit applications together or use the other's assets or income on any application, or make available to the other any credit card associated with separate accounts without getting legal advice first. Married couples attempting to keep separate property separate sometimes run into snags with lenders or title companies if they try to refinance separate real estate.

If a large asset or account is in both names, you would not want to change (transmute) it to a separate property when there is a large debt outstanding or expected, as the change in title could be seen as a transfer to defraud creditors.

There are tax advantages to holding marital property when one spouse dies. For most couples, these and other advantages outweigh the risks. If you are trying to protect yourselves against specific risks by making this kind of agreement, we recommend you get some tax advice about such matters as "stepped-up basis" on marital property on death, and weigh the risks and benefits for yourselves. Like the other financial tailoring examples, this one might sound like a good idea for many people, but it definitely isn't for everyone.

any express designation as beneficiary or to rights as a surviving spouse under Social Security laws or other government benefit or program of assistance.

Explanation

1. The terms and basic effect of the agreement we drafted are intended to keep the property and income of each of us separate, rather than to acquire any marital property. We each want to keep our property separate, and in the event of our death, to leave our property to our respective heirs and not to each other. If we decide to buy property together, it will be owned according to the way we hold title or agree by another written agreement, and there will be no right of reimbursement unless we specifically agree to it in a later written agreement. Neither of us has promised the other anything upon our death. Neither of us will claim we are entitled to anything because of our marital status upon the other's death. The only rights either of us will claim after the other's death will be those, if any, specifically given in writing by the deceased partner. For example, if we open a joint checking account to pay our household expenses and designate it as a joint tenancy account, owned by the survivor upon the death of either of us, we are not waiving our rights to claim such an account after the other's death, since that claim would be based on a specific written agreement, and not on our marital status.

2. By signing this agreement, we are each giving up our right to claim, under any circumstances and at whatever time, that the income, earnings or property of the other partner is marital property. We are each giving up the right to have our children or legal representatives make this kind of claim on our behalf in the event of our death or disability.

Agreement for situation 4

B.   S's house, located at (address), is and will remain her separate property. All property acquired during the marriage, including property held in joint title, will be separate property and not marital property. All income of any nature whatever will be the separate property of the person who earns or receives it and will be kept in separate bank accounts to which the other has no access. Neither party will be responsible for the debts of the other, whether incurred before or during marriage, and each will indemnify, defend and hold harmless the other from any action to collect the one's debts from the other's property, including paying any costs and attorney fees in connection with such an action. We agree to deposit funds from our separate accounts, on an equal basis, in amounts sufficient to pay our joint expenses, into a joint account that will be used only to pay joint expenses.

Explanation

We agree that S's house will remain her separate property, and H's contracting business, (name of business), will remain H's separate property. No marital estate interest will be created in S's separate property or H's separate property by reason of any work or earnings invested in them during the marriage. Everything we acquire during our marriage will be separate property. If we acquire anything in joint title, each of us will own our share of it as separate property, and not as marital property. All income of any nature will also be separate property of the person who earns or receives it. We agree to each be responsible for our own debts and protect the other party from any action to collect the debts of one from the other. By making this agreement, we are each giving up the right to claim a marital property interest in income of the other party. We are each giving up the right to a marital

5. Professional practice or separate business

a. Situation

J operated an accounting practice for ten years prior to his marriage to G. They decide that it would be fair for the practice to remain J's separate property for the first ten years of marriage, but aftwerward, this clause of their agreement will terminate, and the termination will be retroactive so that things will be treated afterward as if this part of their agreement had never been made.

b. Situation

Z is one of numerous officers in a business that his great-grandfather started. He owns a share of the business, as do siblings, uncles, and cousins who also own shares and work in the business, and some who just collect dividends. Since grandfather's time, only direct heirs have been allowed to own shares, with nothing passing to widows, widowers, or divorced spouses. Z is under great pressure to make a premarital agreement to protect the family business and might lose his position and shares without one. Z's fiancée, Y, will be a homemaker. They agree to make things fair by putting 10% of Z's income into Y's separate account.

Comment

In some states, the marital estate can acquire an interest in a separate business to the extent that a spouse's efforts during marriage increase its value. Since that possibility is being given up, the parties here want to do something to make their agreement fair. Premarital agreements have often been made with no effort to balance the equities, which is how they got their bad reputation. There are many ways to make things fair if you want to, depending on the situation of the parties. For example, Z could make Y the beneficiary of a life insurance policy that will be increased a certain amount each year they are married, promising to maintain the policy and keep her or her estate as beneficiary until the day he dies, no matter what. Or, if Y had her own income, retirement and stock options, they could agree to make that entirely her own separate property. In situations like this, we strongly urge you to use independent counsel for both parties to negotiate and draft the financial part of your agreement.

property interest in any assets that might be acquired by the other party or in which work or earnings might be invested during our marriage. We are each undertaking an obligation to protect and defend the other party's income and assets from any debts that we might incur. We are both obligated to share equally any joint expenses.

Agreement for situation 5(a)

B.   The marital estate will acquire no ownership or interest in J's accounting practice or in any increase in value it might enjoy, no matter how much time or effort either of us might devote to it. If J sells his practice or exchanges it for another asset, the proceeds or acquired asset will also be J's separate property. The agreement in this paragraph will automatically terminate ten years from the date it becomes effective and our rights and obligations will be governed by other provisions of this agreement as if this paragraph had never existed.

Explanation

By this agreement, G is giving up any right to claim that the marital estate has acquired an interest in J's accounting practice or in proceeds if J sells it or exchanges it for some other asset, no matter how much effort either party puts into it. However, if we are still together in ten years, this paragraph will terminate and the marital estate will retroactively acquire the interest in J's accounting practice it would have acquired if this clause of our agreement had never existed.

Agreement for situation 5(b)

B.   Y agrees that the marital estate will not for any reason or under any circumstances acquire an interest in Z's shares in his family business, ZeeCorp, which will remain Z's own separate property. In exchange, Z agrees that at the end of each calendar year, starting December 31, 2007, he will deposit 10% of his net annual after-tax income into Y's separate account, to be transmuted into Y's separate property, and neither Z nor the marital estate will have a right to reimbursement for the sums deposited.

Explanation

By signing this agreement, Y agrees that the marital estate cannot acquire any interest in Z's shares in ZeeCorp, his family business, and that Z will make annual deposits of 10% of his net after-tax income into Y's separate account, starting December 31, 2007. Y is giving up the right to claim a marital property interest in Z's shares in ZeeCorp, and Z is giving up the right to reimbursement to himself or the marital estate for sums transmuted to Y's separate property by operation of this clause.

6. Staying home to care for child, parent or disabled family member

Situation

Z is quitting a solid career to stay home and care for C, Y's injured child, Z's stepchild. This means giving up seniority, retirement benefits, earnings and opportunities for promotion for what might take a couple of years. The couple feel something should be done to balance the equities and compensate Z for the sacrifice.

Comment

The obligation of care is inherent in the relationship, so you can't agree to compensate someone for caring for his/her own child or, after you're already married, caring for the other spouse. However, it is okay to agree *before* marriage to compensation for the care of a spouse because no obligation exists at that time. In this case, the care is for a stepchild to whom no inherent duty of care is owed, so compensation is permitted and Y has separate funds to pay it. Depending on your situation, you could make a gift to the caregiver of some marital property without right to reimbursement. There could be tax consequences, so check first with a tax accountant.

7. Anticipation of a significant inheritance

Situation

F and J have cared for F's aged mother, M, for several years with most of the burden falling on J, but saving the family the expense of professional care. They agree that J's efforts are worth at least $2,000 per month, so whenever M dies, J can choose either to have any gifts or inheritance F gets from M be treated as marital rather than separate property or to have F pay to J from his separate funds an amount equal to $2,000 for each month she cared for M.

8. Honoring personal preferences over state law

Situation

H and S are fiercely competitive executives. They want all their assets and earnings to be separate property and kept separately, but they will contribute equally (or in proportion to their previous years' net income) into a joint account to cover expenses. However, they plan to buy a house and make some joint

Agreement for situation 6

B.   In consideration of Z having quit a stable career in order to stay home and care for C, Y's child and Z's stepchild, and thus giving up seniority, retirement contributions, earnings, and opportunities for promotion and advancement, Y agrees: (1) on signing of this agreement, Y will pay $5,000 of Y's separate funds into Z's separate account, and (2) on the last day of each month, or portion of a month, that Z continues to care for C, Y will pay $2,500 from Y's separate account into Z's separate account. All such funds will be transmuted into Z's separate property and Y waives all rights and claims that he and the marital estate might have to reimbursement of those funds.

Explanation

Because Z is abandoning a successful career to care for Y's child, C, we agree that Y will deposit funds from Y's separate account into Z's separate account and make monthly deposits as long as Z continues to care for C. Y understands that by this agreement he is giving up the right to keep the agreed amount as his own separate property.

Agreement for situation 7

B.   Since May 2002, most of the burden of caring for F's mother, M, during her declining years has fallen on J. We agree therefore that when M dies, J can choose either (1) to have the entire amount of any gift or inheritance that F receives from M transmuted into our marital property no matter when it is received, or (2) to have F pay to J from his separate funds, to be transmuted into her separate property, an amount equal to $2,000 for each month between May 2002 and M's demise.

Explanation

I, F, understand that when my mother passes away, I will, at J's option, be either (1) giving up the right to keep any gift or inheritance from my mother as my separate property, or (2) paying to J, as her separate property, an agreed amount from my separate funds. I feel this is fair because the care J has given my mother is worth more than the agreed amount and has saved my mother and us the considerable expense of nursing home care. My mother's estate would be much less if not for J's help.

Agreement for situation 8

B.   Except as otherwise specified in this agreement, we agree that:

1.   During our marriage all gifts, inheritances, and earned and unearned income whenever received, will be the separate property of the person who earns or receives it.

2.   All property acquired during our marriage will be separate property, so long as it is kept in separate accounts or separate title. All income and appreciation flowing from separate property will remain separate. Property without title will be the separate property of the person who paid for it.

3.   Any property or accounts that we intend to own jointly will be owned according to how the title or account is held.

investments together, and if they ever have a child together, they understand that keeping everything separate won't be appropriate. Married couples attempting to keep separate property separate sometimes run into problems with lenders or title companies if they try to refinance separate property.

E.   How to add clauses to your basic agreement

To tailor financial relationships, you just add clauses under existing sections of the basic agreement, mostly section 6, which starts out like this:

6.   Money, property and financial matters

A.   Except as modified by this agreement, we agree that all of our mutual rights and obligations with respect to our marital and financial affairs, including our income, debts, and property, will be governed by the laws of _____, no matter where we might live in the future.

Label the first basic clause "A," as shown. Each clause you add will then be labeled B, C, D, etc., in order, depending on how many you use.

Married? If you're not yet married, you should define your premarital assets and debts and what will become of them after marriage. If you're already married, you can still clarify the ownership of assets and debts by defining which are separate and which are marital and what's to become of the profits and proceeds.

Schedules. Whenever you are dealing with more than a few items of property in any clause, rather than list them all in your agreement, you can attach lists at the back of the agreement and label them Schedule 1, 2, etc. This makes it easier to add or delete items without having to rewrite the entire agreement. The particular number you use will depend on whatever other sechedules have come before it in your agreement. In our example, Exhibit A is always the Nolo Supplementary Family Arbitration Rules, and Schedules 1 and 2 are the financial disclosures of the two parties, which are used if you do disclosure.

Termination. Don't forget that any clause can be made to terminate on a specific date or condition—say, when debts are paid off or if a child is born or adopted—in which case you must decide if the termination is (a) retroactive to the beginning, so things become as if the clause never existed, or (b) not retroactive, leaving everything as it was on the day the clause terminated. See situation 8 in section D above.

Get help. These examples and solutions are relatively simple. Unless your situation and tailoring efforts are fairly straightforward and similarly simple, we

4. We will deposit into a joint account equal amounts of money from our separate accounts, sufficient to pay our joint expenses. The joint account will be used only to pay joint expenses.

5. Nothing in the above paragraphs should be construed to restrict anyone's right to make a gift or to voluntarily spend additional separate funds on joint expenses, and there will be no right to an accounting to equalize contributions from past months.

6. In the event that we adopt or have a child born to us,
(a) clauses B1, B2 and B3 will automatically terminate and have no further effect. From that time forward our property rights and duties will be governed by state law and the other clauses of this agreement. The termination will not be retroactive, so that all property and debts defined as separate by this agreement will remain separate; and,
(b) we will each transfer into our marital estate, and transmute into marital property, funds or assets equal to 25% of our respective net worth with no right of reimbursement.

C. We will each be responsible for our separate debts, whether incurred before or during our marriage, and debts incurred in connection with our separate affairs. We will each indemnify, defend and hold harmless the other from any action to collect the one's debts from the other's property, including paying any costs and attorney fees in connection with such an action.

Explanation

By making this agreement, we are each giving up our right to have earnings during our marriage become marital property. If we want anything we own to become marital property, we will change its ownership (transmute it) in writing. We will each contribute equal amounts to family living expenses, but anything either of us earns beyond that amount will belong to the person who earned it, to do with as he or she pleases.

We each have the right to decide to spend extra separate funds on joint expenses without any right to demand later that it be made equal. For example, if one of us wishes to pay the entire cost of a vacation or buy something extra for both of us out of our own funds, the other will not have to contribute an equal amount. We are both able to earn a good income, and we think it is fair for each of us to have complete ownership and control over whatever each of us earns beyond paying our half of our monthly living expenses, so long as we don't have children together.

We do not know whether we will have children in the future. If we do, we are agreeing that we will then each keep 75% of our separate property and contribute 25% of our net worth to the marital estate, and after that, whatever each of us earns will be marital property as it would be under the laws of _____ if we married on that date without an agreement. We think this is fair because if we become parents we want the flexibility to curtail either of our careers for the sake of the family and share everything either of us earns equally. We also understand that we would not otherwise be obligated to give any of our separate property to the marital estate, so if we have a child together, we are giving up the right to keep our separate property separate to the extent of 25% of our net worth on that date.

urge you to have a family law attorney review financial and parenting terms of your agreement (see chapter 3B).

F. How to do financial disclosure

If you decide to do any tailoring of financial relationships in your agreement, then well before your agreement is signed you must—repeat, *must*—make a full and fair disclosure to each other of your finances, which means to exchange a written list of all your assets and their values, amounts owed, and your annual income. The purposes for doing this are (1) to make sure both parties have the opportunity to understand both the agreement and the financial affairs of both parties sufficiently well to make a sound decision; (2) to allow you or your executor to sort out separate from marital assets and debts in the future; and (3) to withstand scrutiny if one party later claims they were misled or not given accurate or sufficient information.

So, no less than seven days before you sign your agreement, you must each receive a copy of the final agreement and a written explanation of the agreement (chapter 8) and, at the same time or earlier, you must each present the other with a list of your financial information—the disclosure. The waiting period is to show that you both had time to consider the final agreement and the background financial information before deciding to sign. How to do disclosure is explained in this section.

Disclosure worksheets. To do disclosure, you must each prepare a written list of all your assets and their values, amounts owed, and your annual income. To help you organize this information, and as a checklist to make sure you haven't overlooked anything, we've prepared a disclosure worksheet that you'll find on the companion CD. There is also a Simplified Schedule that you can use if you prefer.

The disclosure statement. For the actual written disclosure, you can use either a completed Disclosure Worksheet or the Simplified Schedule, one for each of you. Both are on the companion CD. The Simplified Schedule is illustrated on the next page. However you do it, the information you present to each other must be attached to your agreement as Schedules 1 and 2 to show what was disclosed.

Schedule 1
Financial Information of Chris Brown

ASSETS

Description	Approximate value
Residence at 123 4th Street, Santa Theresa, CA	$325,000
Savings account at Wells Fargo, Santa Theresa, CA	8,325
1998 Toyota Corolla, CA lic. no. 3XYZ123	2,500
Household furniture and personal possessions	6,000
Computer and other electronics	1,200

DEBTS

Owed to	Approximate balance due
First mortgage on residence at 123 4th Street, Santa Theresa, CA	$180,000
Line of credit on residence at 123 4th Street, Santa Theresa, CA	21,000
Master Card	2,200
Hi-Tech Emporium	450

Approximate annual income: $42,575

Approximate annual expenses: $38,250

Date:

_____
Chris Brown

Schedule 1   Page 1 of 1

Detail. Valuable assets like real estate, businesses, savings accounts, retirement funds, vehicles, and the like should be listed and valued separately, as should anything of special significance to you, no matter how much it costs. Likewise, obligations like mortgages, bank loans and large credit card debts should be listed separately. However, for all the stuff in between, you can lump things together in categories, like household furnishings, tools, jewelry, computers and electronics, etc.

Values. Valuations in modest estates can cost little or nothing: get values from similar properties for sale in newspaper, penny-saver classifieds, or on eBay, and so on. Cars can be valued for free on the Kelley Bluebook Web site at www.kbb.com. If you have little equity in a home, ask a real estate agent for current values. However, as an asset's worth increases, the need to be more accurate also increases. If you have a lot of equity in a home, a professional real estate appraisal would be worth getting for a few hundred dollars. Businesses are famously difficult to value and appraisals are not only very expensive, they are not particularly reliable. So, instead of valuing a business, make a statement that says what kind of business it is, the value of its assets (such as equipment and accounts receivable), how long it has been operating and how much money it earns per year. Also say how it is organized—partnership, a corporation, sole proprietorship, or some other kind of organization. If it's a partnership or corporation, state your share of ownership. This is enough information for your partner to get advice about its potential value. If your partner asks for more information, give it to them. If you are already married when you sign an agreement, you *have* to let your spouse see all the books if they ask.

Valuing retirement funds that are similar to savings accounts, like a 401k plan, just requires a look at the latest statement to know how much is in the fund. However, defined benefit plans, where you don't get anything until you retire, are a can of worms and must be valued by a qualified pension plan actuary. If you haven't many years invested in the plan, just use the plan statement with a note that says you're not sure of the true value but have x years contributing to it. However, if you have quite a few years, you might have to get an appraisal.

Credit history. If your credit is pretty good, no need to say anything about it, but you should provide information about bad credit, unpaid debts, lawsuits, judgments, bankruptcies, or the like. It is relatively easy to order a copy of your own credit report either on the Internet or from any credit reporting agency, which you could attach to your disclosure. If one of you is in a large-size business, you might also include a report from Dun and Bradstreet.

Replace section 7 in the basic agreement. Because you are doing disclosure, you need to replace section 7 of the basic agreement (waiver of disclosure) with language confirming that each of you fully disclosed financial information to the other. Here below is the language you will now be using instead of that shown in chapter 2:

7. Disclosures

Each of us has made a full, fair and reasonable disclosure to the other of annual income, all assets owned and all obligations owed on the date such information was presented.

Chris' income, assets owned and obligations owed are set forth in Schedule 1, which is attached to and made part of this agreement. [**Optional:** Attached to Schedule 1 is/are the following additional document(s:) ☐ Chris's federal and/or state tax return for years (years) ☐ the following appraisals: (name them) ☐ other (specify).]

Jamie's income, assets owned and obligations owed are set forth in Schedule 2, which is attached to and made part of this agreement. [**Optional:** Attached to Schedule 2 is/are the following additional document(s:) ☐ Jamie's federal and/or state tax return for years (years) ☐ the following appraisals: (name them) ☐ other (specify).]

We each understand that values set forth in Schedules 1 and 2 are approximate values on the date presented, estimated to the best of our ability, but not necessarily exact.

I, Chris, received a copy of Schedule 2 and any attached documents indicated above on (date), and reviewed that information before signing this agreement. I consider this information to be sufficient and am satisfied with the information I have received.

I, Jamie, received a copy of Schedule 1 and any attached documents indicated above on (date), and reviewed that information before signing this agreement. I consider this information to be sufficient and am satisfied with the information I have received.

Attach to agreement. To show what disclosure has been given, you will attach copies of each party's disclosure documents to your agreement, labeled as Schedules 1 and 2.

G. Estate matters

The Couples Contract is forward-thinking; planning for a lasting future. So is estate planning. Estate planning is about providing for the future with things like durable powers of attorney for health care and finances, wills, living trusts and other ways to avoid probate and taxes. This is not only beyond the scope of this book, but we think estate planning is generally best done outside your relationship agreement. We think it best not to include estate planning terms in your Couples Contract unless recommended by a certified financial planner or an estate planning professional, who would supply recommended language. Nolo has several excellent estate planning books and some articles to help you get pointed in the right direction at www.nolo.com.

Read more. An article about inheritance and the rights of surviving spouses appears in the Legal Briefs folder on the companion CD.

Health care planning. We think everyone should create a Health Care Directive as soon as possible. This is a very important, useful document and something you can easily do yourself. It typically has two parts: the first lets you name one or more individuals to make medical decisions for you if you are unable to do so, and the second part lets you declare in advance how you would like to be treated medically in case you are unable to speak for yourself. The form can be slightly different for each state, but should be fairly easy to find for free or nearly so. Call and ask at any nearby hospital or large health clinic as they often have them available, or ask your doctor, or go on the Internet and search for "Health Care Directive" (with the quotes) plus the name of your state.

CHAPTER

6

Variations for a faith-based agreement

In recent years, few issues in the United States have been so controversial and divisive as those related to "family values." While partisans launch lawsuits and political campaigns, many religious leaders have come to believe it is better for each faith to govern its own families rather than struggle for legislation to make state laws match their beliefs and values. They wonder if the ancient tradition of marriage contracts can be resurrected to achieve this goal. We think they can.

A. Religious contracts and the faith-based agreement

Covenant, Ketubah, or Aqd. Some religions make signing a marriage contract part of the marriage ritual. These contracts might be just between the couple or they might also involve their families and other members of the community. In a wedding "after the manner of Friends" (Quaker), the bride and groom recite vows to each other, sign their marriage certificate, then the guests sign as witnesses. In traditional Jewish weddings, the bride and groom sign a *Ketubah*, which is often written in elaborate calligraphy, framed and hung in the couple's home. An Islamic *Aqd* is signed by the groom and an adult male member of the bride's family as her agent, or by the bride herself. Other faiths also have their own versions of the religious marriage contract.

    Unenforceable in court. While these may be referred to as contracts, and may even contain contract language, it is important to understand that state courts probably won't treat them that way. The couple might think of them as legally binding, as might courts in other countries, but the law of the land requires separation of church and state, so judges will typically regard religious marriage contracts as inherently religious in nature and not something they have the power to enforce (see section C below).

    The faith-based agreement. If you really want your marriage to be governed by the laws of your faith rather than state law, you will need to sign a separate agreement that looks like a contract to lawyers and judges. This is what we mean by a faith-based agreement. By adding clauses like those described below to our Couples Contract, a couple can pledge to maintain their family according to the beliefs of their faith, to raise their children in the faith, and to submit any family problems or disputes to conciliation, mediation, and arbitration within the faith community.

B. Pros and cons

Not many subjects these days are without controversy, and this is no exception. Many religious organizations are eager to keep the problems of their families within the bosom of the faith community. More, they would like to counsel, mediate and, if all else fails, arbitrate according to the beliefs of their faith rather than the laws of the state. This is certainly understandable and even laudable, but not without risk and not without some dissenting opinion. For example, this news story from The West Australian printed January 5, 2004:

> Father Joe Parkinson, head of the Catholic Church's L. J. Goody Bioethics Centre, said a legal contract that took effect when a marriage ended was contrary to the Christian understanding of marriage. "An unconditional commitment is at the very heart of the Christian understanding of marriage," he said.

And, referring to prenuptial contracts as "prenups," Rabbi Shmuley Boteach, wrote in his Internet "Kosher Coupling" column at www.beliefnet.com:

> Those who insist on prenups are more interested in money than in love. They think that since what motivates them is financial, the same must be true for everybody else. We do not ask a spouse to sign an agreement that they will look after us in our old age, or that they will stay with us if we fall sick or lose our looks. A commitment that transcends such superficiality is implied in the vows we take when we marry. We trust these things will come to pass based on the character of the mate we have chosen and not by a document they have signed.

Of course, these good clergymen were thinking of the traditional prenuptial contract and didn't know about our kinder-gentler Couples Contract, which does not include provisions that specifically anticipate separation. On the other hand, our clause that refers all disputes to mediation and arbitration could certainly be called into play if one party wants to end the relationship.

Our concern goes to who, exactly, in your faith community will undertake mediation and who will be the arbitrator, empowered to make final decisions regarding property, support, custody and parenting. Not just anyone can do these demanding jobs: they require training, knowledge, experience and skill. Will your conciliator be trained in couple counseling? Will your mediator have the training and experience it takes to do a good job? Will your arbitrator be familiar with state family law? Will that person be intolerant and decide punitively toward a spouse who wants to separate or leave the fold? Is the faith community large enough and does it contain a talent pool of qualified leaders who could be fair to parties who have developed divergent views?

Agreeing to have marital matters decided by a member of a faith community can expose parties to decisions by a person not familiar or sympathetic with state family law, or not skilled at dealing with couples in opposition, and there is no provision in these agreements to protect a spouse who, years later, becomes disillusioned and wants to leave the fold, or who converts to another faith.

Many faith communities recognize these problems, too, and are taking steps toward developing recognized bodies of talented people trained to work with these kinds of issues, even developing model agreements for their members to sign, but most are just getting started. Unless your faith community has an established organization with recognized procedures for resolving family disputes, you take a risk putting the decision-making power that goes along with a binding arbitration agreement in their hands. On the other hand, families who are deeply religious may still trust their faith community more than they trust the civil courts to make decisions, if necessary, on a basis that is consistent with their values.

Our personal preference and strong recommendation to you at this time would be to have your faith agreement provide for religious conciliation and mediation only—but do not refer arbitration to your faith community unless your faith group is affiliated with a large organization that provides well-established religious court or arbitration services by people who are trained and certified for the job. As more and more religious organizations develop these resources, you can modify your agreement later to add faith-based binding arbitration to your agreement. Another option we provide says you will use a panel of three arbitrators, one of whom is appointed by your faith community. This allows matters of faith to be an important part of the decision-making process, but eliminates most of the risks that concern us, described above.

As faith-based groups begin to consider these issues and look for better ways to resolve family problems within their communities, several of them have developed model agreements tailored to their faith. However, laws that deal with relationship agreements vary greatly from one state to another, and the model agreements we have seen might be difficult to enforce in some states. At the end of this chapter, we reproduce two model agreements that have been endorsed by religious organizations and discuss the problems we see with trying to enforce them. If your faith community endorses a model agreement, we recommend you read the sections where we talk about these, and compare the model you are given with the basic agreement in this book. You will need both legal and religious advice to modify another organization's relationship agreement to make certain it is enforceable in your state. Talk to your religious advisor, then discuss your proposed agreement with a family law attorney.

Resources. Take a look at the Peacemaker Ministries and Institute for Christian Conciliation at www.HisPeace.org and see their Rules for Christian Conciliation. For another flavor, see the Beth Din organization at www.bethdin.org, where arbitrators are available to render decisions according to Jewish principles, or search the Internet under "Beit Din" or "Bet Din" for some others. Then there's the highly regarded Marriage Encounter, which offers nationwide programs for troubled marriages that are "based on Judeo-Christian concepts. You can get more information about them at www.marriage-encounter.org.

We searched but were unable to find similar resources for other faith organizations. If you know of any, please let us know. We encourage the creation of resources for marriage contracts and conciliation, mediation and arbitration services in all faith communities and would be pleased to consult with any who wish to do so.

Caution! Please, before you decide to make a faith-based agreement, take this book to the leadership of your religious community and discuss the ideas in it. Ask if they have leaders in your community with couples-communication training, or mediators and arbitrators who are also family law attorneys or otherwise qualified to decide a couple's rights under such an agreement. Perhaps they have already developed some contract language of their own, in which case you should get advice from a family law attorney (chapter 3B) about their language.

C. Enforcement

A few states—notably New York, Delaware, and Illinois—have enforced certain religious provisions of premarital contracts under some circumstances. But, because the federal Constitution and those of many states require separation of church and state, most courts will typically ignore agreements about religious matters. However, arbitrators might enforce portions of your agreement that a court could not or would not; so, if your agreement says all marital disputes will be submitted to arbitration, a court can order you to arbitrate without getting tangled up in religious questions, and the arbitrators don't work for the state, so they can decide the religious questions along with everything else. Courts will never surrender ultimate authority over support or the best interests of children, so faith arbitrators must keep state laws in mind when they make decisions. For example, if an arbitrator were to forbid a child to ever see an otherwise fit parent who left the faith, a court would likely invalidate that part of the decision. This is one reason why the agreement requires your arbitrator, or at least one of them, to have a background in your state's family law.

D. Sample clauses

In this example, the couple belongs to a faith community and would like, as much as legally possible, to keep their relationship, parenting, and other family issues that might arise, within the fold of that community rather than going to outsiders or secular courts. By referring their mediation and arbitration clauses back into their faith community, they maximize the chances that problems in their relationship will be solved according to the principles of their chosen religion. They understand that state courts will never surrender final jurisdiction over support issues or what is in the best interest of any child, but they hope that things will never go that far if the parties accept the decisions of their chosen arbitrator.

Financial matters. Financial matters are discussed in chapter 5, and you use the same clause 6 (financial matters) that is in the basic agreement; but there is also one faith-related variation below in the arbitration section. Please remember, if you tailor financial rights in your agreement, you have to do full disclosure as described in chapter 5F.

Faith-based variations for the basic Couples Contract

Paragraph numbers below refer to paragraphs in the basic agreement (chapter 2) that you can modify as shown here.

Title. While you can title your agreement almost anything you want, it would be best to avoid a title that makes it appear that the agreement is fundamentally religious.

4. Principles for a lasting marriage. You are free to treat this section of the basic agreement any way you like: keep it as it is, add to it, modify it, or do it the way we suggest in this example.

Variations for a faith-based basic Couples Contract

2. Commitments

(after the existing first paragraph, add the following:)

We agree that our religious faith and relationships in our faith community are fundamental and that we will establish a household and a family that will live in accord with the beliefs of the (name) faith. We agree to maintain our membership in (name) or another similar faith community, should we move or mutually decide to change our religious affiliation. We agree to attend religious services regularly together. We agree that any children that may be born to us or adopted by us will be raised in the (name) faith and that we will observe the practices of that faith in our home.

4. Principles for a lasting marriage

It is our intention to create a lasting marriage based upon mutual respect, affection and friendship, and the principles of marriage taught by our faith. Should issues ever arise between us that threaten to undermine our closeness and mutual regard, we agree to take steps together to improve our relationship with the help and guidance of our faith community, including, if available, counseling and conciliation programs.

[Continue with any other clauses from the basic agreement that you want to keep or adapt.]

5. Parenting

[add this paragraph at the end of the paragraphs in the basic agreement]

We agree that any children that may be born to us or adopted by us will be raised in the (name) faith and that we will observe the practices of that faith in our home for their benefit as well as our own.

9. Resolution of disputes—mediation and arbitration

A. Mediation

If we are unable to resolve any dispute privately, then on the written request of either party, within thirty days we will submit our dispute to mediation with a mediator agreed upon by both of us. Unless we agree otherwise, our mediator must be a member of (faith community) and preferably a family law attorney who specializes in family law mediation in the state named in clause 10D or, if such is not available, someone who has experience with family mediation. If we are unable to agree on a mediator, we agree that

☐ we will each choose one person within our faith community and those two persons together will appoint our mediator.

☐ the (rabbi/pastor/elders/other appropriate title) of (faith community), or of the faith community we both belong to at the time of the dispute, may appoint a mediator to help us resolve our dispute. If we are not at that time members of the same faith community, the mediator will be appointed by the rabbi/pastor/elders of the last faith community we both belonged to.

We will participate in mediation in good faith and pay the cost of mediation from community funds, if available, and if community funds are not available, we will each be responsible for half the cost of such mediation.

B. Arbitration

1.   In the event that mediation does not resolve the issue within a reasonable number of sessions, then upon the written request of either party, we will submit the matter to binding arbitration within thirty days. Our arbitrator must be a family law professional in the state named in clause 10D: an attorney who specializes in mediation or arbitration, or a retired family court judge, with preference given to one who is a member of our faith community. The arbitrator will be agreed upon by both of us. If we are unable to agree on an arbitrator,

☐ we will each choose one person within our faith community and those two persons together will appoint an arbitrator who meets our agreed qualifications.

☐ the (rabbi/pastor/elders/other appropriate title) of (faith community), or of the faith community we both belong to at the time of the dispute, may appoint an arbitrator who meets our agreed qualifications. If we are not at that time members of the same faith community, the arbitrator will be appointed by the (rabbi/pastor/elders) of the last faith community we both belonged to.

☐ the matter will be arbitrated by a panel of three arbitrators. We will each choose one arbitrator without regard to professional qualification, and our two arbitrators together will appoint the third arbitrator, who must be an experienced family law attorney who specializes in mediation and arbitration, or a retired family court judge.

2.   If we use a single arbitrator, we will pay the cost of arbitration from community funds, if available, and if community funds are not available, we will each be responsible for half the cost of the arbitration. If we use a panel of three arbitrators, each of us will pay the fees of the arbitrator we appoint. The fees of the third arbitrator will be paid from community funds, if available, and if community funds are not available, we will each be responsible for half the fees of the third arbitrator and other costs of arbitration.

3.   We are each entitled to representation in arbitration by an attorney of our choice. Attorney fees will be ☐ borne by each party separately. ☐ paid from community funds, if available, and if community funds are not available, each party will be responsible for his or her own attorney's fees.

4.   The arbitrator(s) will have the power to interpret the terms of this agreement, decide questions of their own jurisdiction, and settle disputes arising between the parties regarding the arbitrability of claims and the interpretation of the agreement. The arbitrator(s) will not have the power to alter, modify or terminate any provision of this agreement. The arbitration will be conducted under

☐ rules to be agreed upon by the arbitrator(s) and the parties, but if there is no consensus, the rules will be determined by the arbitrator(s).

☐ the arbitration rules of (faith-based organization).

In any event, the parties agree they will adopt and apply the Nolo Supplementary Family Arbitration Rules, a copy of which is attached to this Agreement as Exhibit A.

5. **Arbitration is binding and final.** The decision of the arbitrator(s) will be binding and final, not subject to review in any court. We each understand that by agreeing to binding arbitration, we are choosing arbitration as the sole remedy for any dispute between us, and we each expressly give up our right to file a lawsuit or family law proceeding in any court against one another, or to request a court to resolve any dispute between us, except to compel arbitration or enforce the decision of an arbitrator. We understand that this means we are giving up the right to trial by a court or jury. To whatever extent the law does not allow any issue between us to be decided by binding arbitration, we agree to submit such matters to nonbinding arbitration before submitting the issue to any court.

[Optional]

6. If an action is required to enforce the use of binding arbitration required by this agreement, or the decision of an arbitrator, the costs and expenses of the prevailing party in such judicial proceeding, including, but not limited to, his or her reasonable attorney's fees, will be paid by the unsuccessful party.

Optional provision for children

6. We agree that if we should ever separate, the arbitrator(s) may decide custody, visitation and support issues for any children we may have together and, in making such decisions, the arbitrator(s) may consider any factors that may be just and fair, keeping the best interests of the children uppermost. The arbitrator(s) may consider, among all other factors affecting the children's welfare, each parent's willingness and ability to continue to raise the children according to our agreement about their religious upbringing. Nothing in this agreement shall be construed to adversely affect the right to support of any child.

Optional provision for faith-based division of property

6. We agree that if we separate or it appears necessary to the arbitrator(s) for us to separate, the arbitrator(s) may divide our marital property equitably between us. In making such division, the arbitrator(s) may consider any factors that may be just and fair according to the laws and principles of the (name) faith. We each specifically waive our right to have our property divided according to state law.

Variation for faith-based division of property

Comment on the last optional clause on the previous page. Some religions have their own well-defined rules about property rights upon divorce and a religious court capable of dividing their property. If you add this clause at the end of section 9, it gives the arbitrator authority to divide property according to the rules of your religion rather than state law. However, you'll have to careful, because if your state's public policy favors no-fault divorce, courts might not enforce a decison based on an agreement that *explicitly* penalizes a spouse for marital misconduct. Discuss this with a family law attorney in your faith community if this is what you want to do.

    Caution! This kind of financial agreement requires a high degree of trust in the rules, systems and arbitrators in your religious community. Few religious organizations have enough of a track record to allow you to predict what would happen in case you ever need to rely on them to apply this clause. Even fewer have rules and procedures that allow a bad decision to be appealed. It makes divorce or separation a much more risky prospect, which might be what your religious leaders want, but is it really what you want?

    A variation would be to say that the arbitrators "must divide our marital property in a fair and substantially equal manner." This is similar to the current laws of many other states where precise mathematical equality is not required, but the decision makers are not given a blank check to do anything they think is right.

Alternative dispute resolution clauses from Peacemaker Ministries

Frankly, we are partial to our own language, but here below, for comparison, are clauses that bring the agreement under the Rules of Procedure for Christian Conciliation. Do **not** sign either of these clauses without carefully studying the Rules referred to, which are on the companion CD that comes with this book.

The new language would be used in place of both 9A and 9B in the basic Couples Contract.

9. Resolution of disputes

Any claim or dispute arising from or related to this agreement shall be settled by mediation and, if necessary, legally binding arbitration in accordance with the *Rules of Procedure for Christian Conciliation* of the Institute for Christian Conciliation, a division of Peacemaker® Ministries (complete text of the Rules is available at www.HisPeace.org). Judgment upon an arbitration decision may be entered in any court otherwise having jurisdiction. The parties understand that these methods shall be the sole remedy for any controversy or claim arising out of this agreement and expressly waive their right to file a lawsuit in any civil court against one another for such disputes, except to enforce an arbitration decision.

They also offer this clause:

9. Resolution of disputes

The parties to this agreement are Christians and believe that the Bible commands them to make every effort to live at peace and to resolve disputes with each other in private or within the Christian church (see Matthew 18:15-20; 1 Corinthians 6:1-8). Therefore, the parties agree that any claim or dispute arising from or related to this agreement shall be settled by biblically based mediation and, if necessary, legally binding arbitration in accordance with the *Rules of Procedure for Christian Conciliation* of the Institute for Christian Conciliation, a division of Peacemaker® Ministries (complete text of the Rules is available at www.HisPeace.org). Judgment upon an arbitration decision may be entered in any court otherwise having jurisdiction. The parties understand that these methods shall be the sole remedy for any controversy or claim arising out of this agreement and expressly waive their right to file a lawsuit in any civil court against one another for such disputes, except to enforce an arbitration decision.

Caution! If you decide to use one of these clauses, or a similar one from another organization, be sure to find out if the rules are designed for family disputes that might require emergency orders for child custody and support while waiting for the arbitrator to be chosen, or modification of child custody and child or spousal support after arbitration if circumstances change. Unless the organization has a set of rules specifically designed to handle these matters in family disputes, we recommend you add this language immediately after naming the rules of your organization: "as modified by Nolo Supplementary Family Arbitration Rules, a copy of which is attached to this Agreement."

E. Other religious marriage contracts

Two large faith-based dispute resolution organizations, the Peacemaker Ministries and Beth Din of America, have pioneered the concept of faith-based marriage agreements for Christian and Jewish couples, respectively. We include their model agreements here, and describe the problems we see with enforcing them.

As other religious organizations follow suit and publish recommended relationship agreements, we will post links to them on our Web site at www.nolocouples.com. If your faith community has experience with marriage contracts, please let us know so we can post your information there, too.

1. Peacemaker Ministries

Many Christians are strongly opposed to divorce on moral grounds. As the divorce rate has climbed over the last 50 years, many Christian organizations have looked for ways to reverse the trend and help keep Christian couples together. Some have advocated elimination of no-fault divorce, at least for some couples. The states of Louisiana, Arizona and Arkansas have enacted covenant-marriage laws. These laws generally require couples to have a certain amount of premarital counseling and to sign an agreement to have their marriage governed by a different set of laws, similar to the old fault-based divorce laws, making it more difficult for them to get a divorce. It is doubtful, however, that other state courts will recognize a covenant marriage from another state creating any different rights than normally exist under their own laws.

Peacemaker Ministries has published this model *Marriage Covenant*, which is intended to allow couples to elect a covenant marriage, even in states that do not have a covenant-marriage law. The purpose is to prevent one spouse from demanding a divorce against the wishes of the other spouse and without a good reason. A second purpose is to require both spouses to go to their church for marital help before going to court for a divorce. Our comments about the enforceability of this agreement follow.

Our Marriage Covenant

1.   Believing that God, in His wisdom and providence, has ordained and establishes human marriage as a covenant relationship intended to reflect the eternal marriage covenant established through the death, burial and resurrection of His Son with His Church, and therefore believing that human marriage is a sacred and lifelong promise, reflecting our unconditional love for one another, and believing that God intends for the human marriage covenant to reflect His promise never to leave us or forsake us because of what He has done for us through His Son, Jesus Christ, we, the undersigned husband and wife, male and female, as image of God, do hereby affirm and reaffirm our solemn pledge to fulfill our marriage vows, so help us God.

2.   We furthermore pledge to exalt the sacred nature, glory and permanence of God's eternal marriage covenant in His Son with the Church through our marriage, by calling others to honor and fulfill their marriage vows; and we, upon full and informed consent and with full knowledge and understanding of this covenant and with the intent to enter into and be bound by the terms of this covenant, hereby irrevocably covenant and consent to submit any marital dispute we may have that we cannot resolve and any question concerning whether our marriage should be dissolved to the peacemaking process, including nonbinding Christian mediation and, if necessary, binding arbitration, in accordance with the Rules of Procedure of the Institute for Christian Conciliation, a division of Peacemaker® Ministries (www.HisPeace.org), and under the jurisdiction of our local church of which we are members, or if not members of a local church then under the jurisdiction of any church to which we can agree, but in any event if we cannot reach agreement as to a church for such purposes, then we consent and agree to submit to the peacemaking process as provided in the Rules of Procedure of the Institute for Christian Conciliation, a division of Peacemaker® Ministries, to and including binding arbitration of all matters pertaining to our marriage and family, believing that any and all marital and family disputes and issues involve deeply important religious questions that should be resolved by Christians according to the standards set forth in the Holy Bible, and therefore we do both hereby agree to be bound by any arbitration decision

as to any such dispute or issues concerning our marriage and family, which is made in accordance with the Rules of Procedure of the Institute for Christian Conciliation, a division of Peacemaker® Ministries.

In the presence of God and these witnesses, and by a holy covenant, I, witnesses, and by a holy covenant, I,

_____

Husband's Name
joyfully receive you as God's perfect gift for me, to have and to hold from this day forward, for better, for worse, for richer, for poorer, in sickness and in health, to love you, to honor you, to cherish you and protect you, forsaking all others as long as we both shall live.

_____

Wife's Name
joyfully receive you as God's perfect gift for me, to have and to hold from this day forward, for better, for worse, for richer, for poorer, in sickness and in health, to love you, to honor you, to respect you, forsaking all others as long as we both shall live.

_____

Husband's Signature

_____

Wife's Signature

Witnessed this __ day of _____, by

_____

Witness

_____

Witness

Unless the Lord builds the house, the builders labor in vain. **Psalm 127:1**

Comments

The Covenant is simple and its main points are very similar to our basic Couples Contract after you add the clauses described in this chapter. The first clause of the Covenant is a suitable variation to our section 4—Principles for a lasting marriage. The second clause is similar to our section 9—Resolution of disputes. However, there are several potential problems with enforcing the Covenant in some states.

Unenforceable? It is intended to be signed on the couple's wedding day, during or at the conclusion of the ceremony. Its purpose, according to Peacemaker Ministries, is to make it harder for a Christian marriage to be dissolved at the request of one spouse without "biblical grounds for divorce." Although it contains language about dispute resolution, it makes no mention at all of the usual subjects of a prenuptial agreement—that is, financial or property matters. These characteristics may cause a court to decide it is a religious marriage certificate, not a legally binding prenuptial agreement. Also, if the agreement is signed *after* the marriage ceremony is concluded, it technically is not a *pre*marital contract. Premarital and marital agreements are subject to substantially different laws in many states.

Procedural flaws. Some states have built a tall fence around prenuptial and marital agreements in reaction to many abuses. If you were to sign the Covenant without following all the procedural safeguards recommended for our Couples Contract (financial disclosure plus checklist steps 8 through 11), it is uncertain that it could be enforced.

In a California case,[1] a couple signed an Islamic marriage contract quite similar to this one, in that it said their marriage would be governed "in accordance with his Almighty God's Holy Book and the Rules of his Prophet." It specified the dowry, which is an Islamic marriage custom, but otherwise contained no financial agreements. The court decided it was not a prenuptial agreement, but a marriage certificate, and therefore ignored the part of the agreement that referred to Islamic Law and to the financial dowry. It is possible that had the agreement said all disputes would be resolved by a particular Islamic court, the judge would have viewed it differently, but this is not certain. The absence of any financial terms was a major reason the court decided to ignore it.

---

[1] *In re Marriage of Shaban* (2001) 88 Cal. App. 4th 398

Paragraph 10D of our basic agreement is intended to avoid this problem as simply as possible. It says that no matter where the couple may live, they intend for their property to be community or separate, according to state law.

The third problem with the Covenant is that it says the church will decide "any question concerning whether our marriage should be dissolved." In the material published by Peacemaker Ministries to explain the Covenant, they say that if one spouse files for divorce, the court would stop the divorce case until the church decided this question. We do not believe every (or many) state courts would enforce the Covenant in this way. We think some courts would interpret the Covenant to say the church can decide whether the couple is entitled to a *religious* divorce, but it would have no effect on their *legal* divorce. A court could be persuaded not to decide the financial part of the divorce case when there is a valid arbitration agreement, but will not hand over the power to grant a legal divorce. In most states, no-fault divorce is a matter of public policy. This Covenant does not have a severability clause like paragraph 10A of our Basic Agreement, so it is also possible a court would hold the whole Covenant unenforceable because of this clause.

What's the solution if you belong to a church that is promoting this Covenant? We think you could sign this Covenant at your wedding as a marriage certificate, but sign a separate Couples Contract before the wedding, modeled on our basic agreement with clauses added from this chapter. You can use language copied from the Covenant in paragraphs 4 and 9, and leave out of your agreement the phrase, "whether the marriage should be dissolved."

2. Beth Din of America

Jewish Law, called *Halakha*, gives the husband the right to divorce his wife, but does not give the wife the same right. If the wife obtains a legal divorce, but not a religious divorce, she and her children by a later marriage can be severely penalized within the Jewish faith. A Jewish woman who is legally, but not religiously, divorced is known as an *agunah*, or "chained woman."

In recent years, Jewish communities have seen an increase in the number of women in this situation, and have given considerable attention to finding ways to deal with this problem. One of the leading Orthodox Jewish religious courts, the Beth Din of America, has developed a prenuptial agreement as a possible solution that can be enforced under both American civil law and Jewish law. The purpose of this agreement is to require a separated or divorced Jewish husband and wife to take care of the Jewish religious divorce. This is done by requiring the husband to pay the wife $150 per day from the day they separate until the Jewish divorce is completed. If the wife refuses to cooperate, the husband can have her summoned before the Beth Din and ask them to end his obligation.

In spite of misgivings like those expressed by Rabbi Boteach earlier in this chapter, many rabbis recommend or require couples to make this kind of agreement. In counseling them, they explain to couples that the purpose of the agreement is not so much to plan ahead for their own divorce, but to take a stand against allowing any former husband to make his former wife a "chained woman." In other words, a couple who signs this agreement is making a statement that no Jewish couple should ever treat each other that way, and proving it by their own promises.

THE BETH DIN OF AMERICA
BINDING ARBITRATION AGREEMENT

THIS AGREEMENT MADE ON THE _____ DAY OF THE
MONTH OF _____ IN THE YEAR 20 __, IN THE
CITY/TOWN/VILLAGE OF _____ STATE OF _____.
between:
HUSBAND-TO-BE: _____
RESIDING AT : _____
WIFE-TO-BE: _____
RESIDING AT: _____

The parties, who intend to be married in the near future, hereby agree as follows:
I. Should a dispute arise between the parties after they are married, so that they do not live together as husband and wife, they agree to refer their marital dispute to an arbitration panel, namely, The Beth Din of the United States of America, Inc. (currently located at 305 Seventh Ave., New York, NY 10001, tel. 212 807-9042, www.bethdin.org) for a binding decision.
II. The decision of the Beth Din of America shall be fully enforceable in any court of competent jurisdiction.
III. The parties agree that the Beth Din of America is authorized to decide all issues relating to a *get* (Jewish divorce) as well as any issues arising from this Agreement or the *ketubah* and *tena'im* (Jewish premarital agreements) entered into by the Husband-to-Be and the Wife-to-Be. Each of the parties agrees to appear in person before the Beth Din of America at the demand of the other party.
(Sections IV:A and IV:B are optional. Unless one of these options is chosen, the Beth Din of America will be without jurisdiction to address matters of general financial and parenting disputes between the parties.)

☐ IV:A(1). The parties agree that the Beth Din of America is authorized to decide all monetary disputes (including division of property and maintenance) that may arise between them.

☐ IV:A(2). The parties agree that the Beth Din of America is authorized to decide any monetary disputes (including division of property and maintenance) that may arise between them based on principles of equitable distribution law customarily employed in the United States as found in the Uniform Marriage and Divorce Act.

☐ IV:A(3). The parties agree that the Beth Din of America is authorized to decide any monetary disputes (including division of property and maintenance) that may arise between them based on the principles of community property law customarily employed in the United States as found in the Uniform Marriage and Divorce Act.

☐ IV:B. The parties agree that the Beth Din of America is authorized to decide all disputes, including child custody, child support, and visitation matters, as well as any other disputes that may arise between them.

IV:C. The Beth Din of America may consider the respective responsibilities of either or both of the parties for the end of the marriage, as an additional, but not exclusive, factor in determining the distribution of marital property and maintenance, should such a determination be authorized by Section IV:A or Section IV:B.

V. Failure of either party to perform his or her obligations under this Agreement shall make that party liable for all costs awarded by either the Beth Din of America or a court of competent jurisdiction, including reasonable attorney's fees, incurred by one side in order to obtain the other party's performance of the terms of this Agreement.

VI. The decision of the Beth Din of America shall be made in accordance with Jewish law (*halakha*) or Beth Din ordered settlement in accordance with the principles of Jewish law (*peshara krova la-din*), except as specifically provided otherwise in this Agreement. The parties waive their right to contest the jurisdiction or procedures of the Beth Din of America or the validity of this Agreement in any other rabbinical court or arbitration forum other than the Beth Din of America. The parties agree to abide by the published Rules and Procedures of the Beth Din of America (which are available at www.bethdin.org, or by calling the Beth Din of America) which are in effect at the time of the arbitration. The Beth Din of America shall follow its rules and procedures, which shall govern this arbitration to the fullest extent permitted by law. Both parties obligate themselves to pay for the services of the Beth Din of America as directed by the Beth Din of America.

VII. The parties agree to appear in person before the Beth Din of America at the demand of the other party, and to cooperate with the adjudication of the Beth Din of America in every way and manner. In the event of the failure of either party to appear before the Beth Din of America upon reasonable notice, the Beth Din of America may issue its decision despite the defaulting party's failure to appear, and may impose costs and other penalties as legally permitted. Furthermore, Husband-to-Be acknowledges that he recites and accepts the following:

I hereby now (me'achshav), *obligate myself to support my Wife-to-Be from the date that our domestic residence together shall cease for whatever reasons, at the rate of $150 per day (calculated as of the date of our marriage, adjusted annually by the Consumer Price Index—All Urban Consumers, as published by the U.S. Department of Labor, Bureau of Labor Statistics) in lieu of my Jewish law obligation of support so long as the two of us remain married according to Jewish law, even if she has another source of income or earnings. Furthermore, I waive my* halakhic *rights to my wife's earnings for the period that she is entitled to the above stipulated sum, and I acknowledge that I shall be deemed to have repeated this waiver at the time of our wedding. I acknowledge that I have effected the above obligation by means of a* kinyan *(formal Jewish transaction) in an esteemed* (chashuv) *Beth Din as prescribed by Jewish law.* However, this support obligation shall terminate if Wife-to-Be refuses to appear upon due notice before the Beth Din of America or in the event that Wife-to-Be fails to abide by the decision or recommendation of the Beth Din of America.

VIII. This Agreement may be signed in one or more duplicates, each one of which shall be considered an original.

IX. This Agreement constitutes a fully enforceable arbitration agreement. Should any provision of this Agreement be deemed unenforceable, all other surviving provisions shall still be deemed fully enforceable; each and every provision of this Agreement shall be severable from the other. As a matter of Jewish law, the parties agree that to effectuate this agreement in full form and purpose, they accept now (through the Jewish law mechanism of *kim li*) whatever minority views determined by the Beth Din of America are needed to effectuate the obligations contained in Section VII and the procedures and jurisdictional mandates found in Sections I, II, III and VI of this Agreement.

X. Each of the parties acknowledges that he or she has been given the opportunity prior to signing this Agreement to consult with his or her own rabbinic advisor and legal advisor. The obligations and conditions contained herein are executed according to all legal and *halakhic* requirements.

In witness of all the above, the Husband-to-Be and Wife-to-Be have entered into this Agreement.

SIGNATURE OF HUSBAND-TO-BE: _____

SIGNATURE OF WIFE-TO-BE: _____

WITNESS: _____

WITNESS: _____

Comments

The Beth Din of America agreement is intended to motivate a separated Jewish couple to take care of their religious divorce as quickly as possible. Rabbis and lawyers spent years trying to find a way to do this without violating either state laws or Jewish religious law. The best solution they could find was to require the husband (the one who holds most of the religious rights) to pay the wife $150 per day from the time they separate until they go to the Beth Din for the religious divorce. But this raises a problem because it could be interpreted as a form of spousal support, and some states have limitations on contracts involving spousal support. For example, it would not be enforceable in California unless at least the husband, and preferably also the wife, is represented by an independent attorney.

In addition to Beth Din's provisions for the religious divorce, you could also include other matters from our basic and faith-based agreement. Be sure to get advice from your rabbi about whether anything you want to add will violate Jewish law.

The Beth Din can decide all marital disputes, including property and financial matters, and matters relating to children if you agree, although you must remember that the state court is always the ultimate arbiter of child support and deciding what is in the best interest of a child. The Beth Din of America can decide financial questions according to state law, rather than Jewish law if the couple agrees. They recommend you state specifically whether financial questions are to be decided according to Jewish law or according to state law. Since the law in many states will be quite different from the Jewish marital property system, it is very important that you get specific advice comparing the two systems to help you make the kind of agreement you want. In section D above, we presented a replacement for clause 9 of the basic Couples Contract, to allow arbitrator(s) to divide marital property according to religious law rather than state law.

While the Beth Din attempts to offer services nationally, you need to find out if they are conveniently accessible where you live, so we suggest you consult your rabbi or the Beth Din on this before naming the Beth Din as your arbitrators in your state. Be sure to also inquire about their ability to arbitrate nonreligious issues of a separation or divorce.

Many states do not require this kind of agreement to be witnessed, but since it is intended to be binding under both state law and Jewish law, you should not skip any of the procedures we prescribe for our Couples Contract (financial disclosure plus checklist steps 8–11), or any recommended by your rabbi.

F.   Agreements for interfaith couples

One of the big advantages of the Couples Contract is that the process of making it leads you to clarify your expectations in ways that most couples should but rarely do. For interfaith couples, few things could be more important than to think through and make agreements about how *in practical terms* you plan to blend your two different religious and cultural persuasions into one family life. Of course, we think you should definitely make a Couples Contract to gain all of its benefits, but we don't think your faith-related agreements should be in it.

Here's the problem. The general rule is that lifestyle and religious agreements are not enforceable in court and to include them might cause the entire agreement to fall if a judge finds that they were a substantial basis for making the contract in the first place. This is one reason why we tell you in chapter 2C to put lifestyle agreements in a separate document or letter. However, we draw a distinction and endorse the use of faith-based clauses whenever a couple has access to *trained* mediators and arbitrators in their faith community who can be relied upon to enforce all of their contact fairly. But this solution is not available to interfaith couples, because to use an arbitrator from the faith of one spouse would probably

Illustration courtesy of Interfaith Resources—www.interfaithresources.com

feel unfair to the other. Of course, an arbitrator of any faith, or no faith, is more likely to consider religious and lifestyle agreements than any judge, but you can't be sure about it. So, there is no obvious way that interfaith agreements can be enforced in a Couples Contract in a way that is reassuring to both parties. Therefore, for interfaith couples, we feel you should definitely work out your agreements so you are both clear about your plan and intentions, but put them in a separate document.

Read more. For a more detailed discussion of issues important to interfaith couples, look in the Resources folder on the companion CD for an article very generously contributed by Mary Heléne Rosenbaum, executive director of the Dovetail Institute for Interfaith Family Resources and editor of *Dovetail: A Journal by and for Jewish/Christian Families*. For more information and resources for interfaith couples, go to www.dovetailinstitute.org.

CHAPTER

7

Variations for unmarried couples

Unmarried people[1] living together without a written agreement remind us of those old movies where you see a couple tied up on train tracks with a train bearing down on them from a distance and everyone is riveted by the imminent disaster. The main difference is that in the movies the couple is *aware* of the threat and they *always* get saved. Unmarried couples don't know they're on the tracks, don't know that trains are headed their way, and don't always escape unharmed.

What you don't know *can* hurt you! You need to know that without a written agreement you live in a state of legal and financial ambiguity that is full of risk but has no up side. You are exposed and vulnerable, so that if you don't actually get run over by that train it won't be because of anything you did to avoid it. You need to know that you can protect each other if you write some stuff down. Making agreements is not just about avoiding train wrecks—writing some things down is about getting positive advantages for both of you and for your relationship.

A. Advantages of a written agreement

People fall in love and start living together, working things out as they go along based on affection, trust, and various oral agreements or "understandings" about how bills get paid, who owns the things they buy, and so on. But, unlike married couples, they are regarded by the law in most states as two strangers who share a space. There are no legal definitions for dealing with income, debts, purchases, or any of the things that always come up in any relationship. You have no protections or benefits to fall back on in case of illness, accident or other emergency.

Without a written agreement, you are vulnerable to misunderstanding which can produce friction; or, if upset comes from another quarter, your ambiguous arrangements are subject later to reinterpretation through emotional hindsight. Oral agreements are famously difficult to prove.

---

[1] **Same-sex couples.** In the context of the Couples Contract, legal issues facing unmarried couples are the same, no matter what their sexual orientation. In 3 or 4 states where such unions are recognized, couples who register a Civil Union or Domestic Partnership gain rights almost equivalent to marriage and all discussions in this book addressed to married couples apply equally to them, except for one problem: the likelihood that a sister state will not recognize their relationship if it does not already exist there.

So, it is *very* important to have a written agreement as to who owns what, who pays which debts, and other financial matters. Written agreements prevent arguments and conflict later. Beyond making things clear between you, making your wishes and arrangements known to others can be essential to protecting you and your loved one.

Writing it down for others

a.   Medical emergencies. In case of accident, illness or advanced age, who do you want to step in and take care of you? What happens if you are incapacitated and can't speak for yourself? Without a written document, an unmarried partner has no right to order medical treatment and cannot take charge. He/she might even have trouble getting into a hospital to visit, because, as far as the law is concerned, you two are strangers. However, if you and your partner each sign a simple document called a Health Care Directive, this will solve the problem. See section F9 below.

b.   Financial power of attorney. Similarly, if one of you becomes incapacitated, who will manage your financial affairs? Without written instructions, a family member or your partner will have to go to court for authority. If you each prepare a Durable Power of Attorney for Finances, problem solved. You can give your partner (or other person) authority to do such things as: use your assets to pay bills and ongoing expenses; buy, sell, maintain and pay expenses for real estate; collect Social Security benefits, Medicare, insurance, or the like; invest your assets; buy insurance, file and pay taxes, operate your business, claim inheritances, hire an attorney, and so on. Go to www.nolo.com to find books and software for making such a document.

c.   Creditors. Here's just one example. Let's say your partner holds title to property or an account that you both think belongs in some degree to both of you, but the named owner later goes into debt or runs over someone who sues. Creditors could take the whole asset unless it is clear that you had a prior claim or ownership. Trying to change title after the event looks suspiciously like a transfer to defraud creditors and could land you in a nasty legal squabble. It's best to make everything clear *before* anything happens.

d.   Relatives, friends, business associates. In case anything happens to one of you, a contract is a good way to let everyone else know who owns what and keep the other partner out of unnecessary squabbles.

e. Wills. If an unmarried partner dies without a will, the other partner gets nothing unless there is a contract or some property is held under joint title or in a joint account. It might be possible for the surviving partner to get something anyway, but it would likely involve a long delay and possible struggle in probate court with relatives of the deceased. To protect the surviving partner, you must either make a will, a contract, or both. You can make a contract of the type described in this book, or in Nolo's *Living Together*, which has a wider range of contract clauses and a simple form will as well. Nolo has some excellent books and software for making wills, which you can find at www.nolo.com.

f. Estate planning. Beyond simple wills, you might want to find out how to avoid the delay, trouble and expense of probate by doing estate planning. This would include setting up revocable living trusts, joint accounts with right of survivorship, payable-on-death bank accounts, gifts, joint tenancy in real estate, and the naming of beneficiaries in retirement accounts, securities, investment accounts, and life insurance. Nolo has several excellent software products and books to help you with these matters, which you can find at www.nolo.com.

Writing it down for your own benefit

If you don't expect to be together very long and don't have much in the way of assets, maybe you don't need a written agreement, but everyone else surely does. Here are a few good reasons for writing some things down for your own good:

- You make things clear between you two
- You can introduce ideas that might help your relationship in the future
- You can make your financial relationships more suitable to your situation
- If it ever happened, you'd have a smoother breakup
- You can keep your relationship forever out of court

Unintended implied contracts

In some situations, a contract can be implied from behavior of the parties without being stated in so many words, so it is possible that a court could later find that there was an agreement even if nothing was expressly stated or written down (see F1 below). An important reason for writing things down is to avoid ambiguity that could lead to a fight some day about an agreement that might or might not be reasonably implied from the behavior of the parties. This kind of claim takes a lot of time and energy to prove or disprove. Far better for people who live together if they spell out what they intend in a written agreement, no matter what that is.

B.   Financial clarity

There's much to be gained from writing some things down even if you do not define your financial affairs. The advantages of the basic Couples Contract don't require financial discussions or clarity. So, you can actually accomplish a great deal without much effort or discomfort.

However, failure to define your finances can leave you vulnerable to misunderstanding and unprotected in the event of illness, accident or breakup. If things go bad between you, you can end up in a terrible conflict that could have been avoided. So what's the problem? Why do so many couples prefer having their teeth pulled to talking about money?

All couples, married or not, find it difficult to discuss money, but the problem is especially intense for unmarried couples who typically are not clear about the depth of their commitment. Discussing money can force you to delve into your true feelings and intentions, something that many unmarried couples avoid. Some people are more comfortable if they just ignore the elephant in the room and never mention it. So you're stuck between the desire to protect someone you care about and the fear of having some defining conversations.

Now, a word of hope: for those of you who really are in it for the long haul, experts tell us that working through to financial understanding and agreement can strengthen your relationship. It's one of those things that may not be fun but it's good for you, like exercise and a healthy diet.

1.   What can be done

When thinking about how to tailor financial relationships, these are the things you'll want to think about. Actual contract clauses are described in section F.

   a.   Income. If nothing is defined, all income of any kind belongs to the person who earns or receives it. If you want to pool your incomes, or some of it, in a more committed kind of way, you should make an agreement as to how this will be done. There are two kinds of income to consider: earned income comes from time and effort, while unearned income consists of things like interest, dividends, and rent. You need to define both if both are present in your life.

   b.   Support. There is no legal obligation for one to support the other, but in a long-term relationship you might want to make the commitment to support each other. Or, it might be reasonable for one partner to agree to support the other, either for love or practical considerations, as where one has moved a long distance or given up a good job or career to move in and devote time and energy to the house or to support the business or career of the one paying support. And, unlike married people who can't do it, you are free to agree to support in exchange for services, like housekeeping (but not sex). Similarly, you can agree to take turns supporting each other through years of education, but should say what happens if you break up midway through. If support is in your agreement, you have to decide how long the obligation will continue and what support will include. For example, married couples are expected to support each other after a breakup at a level as close as possible to their lifestyle while together, for at least a long enough time to allow the supported spouse to get back on his or her feet. An unmarried partner can agree to support the other, but in a specific or limited way. You have to define what you intend.

c. **Expenses.** Many couples want to define how expenses get paid, either shared equally or in some proportion, or completely covered by one partner. Without an agreement, there is no clarity as to who is responsible for your joint expenses or how they will get paid.

d. **Debts.** Unless you agree otherwise, debts are owed by the person who incurs them, the one whose name is on the credit card or account. If you have joint income or assets, you need to define how debts get paid. If you pool your income or assets or both, and if one or both of you have separate estates or business, you should agree that joint funds will not be used to pay debts incurred for the benefit of a separate asset or business.

e. **Major assets.** Assets belong to the persons whose names are on the title or account. You can create a joint estate by buying assets in both your names, or simply by transferring assets owned by one of you into a form of co-ownership. If one of you is contributing effort or value to benefit a separate asset of the other, an agreement should be made as to whether or how this will be compensated. You can co-own an asset, such as a house, in equal shares (as joint tenants or tenants in common) or in unequal shares (as tenants in common only). Caution: when the sole owner of an asset conveys title to himself and another person, a gift is made that cannot later be taken back and which could have tax consequences. Check with a professional first!

f. **Income from assets or accounts.** When dealing with an asset, you have to also consider how to treat any income or appreciation that flows from it. Equities can produce dividends; a house can produce rent; intellectual property can be licensed and earn royalties over a long period of time. A house might appreciate in value just by sitting there, or you might put money and effort into fixing it up to increase its value. Unless defined by agreement, all such income belongs to whoever owns the base asset.

g. **Children.** The rights and duties of parents do not depend on whether they are married. Many couples decide to get married when they have a child or start thinking seriously about it. If marriage isn't right for you, an agreement is more important than ever. You will both have obligations to support your child, as well as rights to custody. One of you might qualify for head of household tax filing status by claiming the child as a dependent, but you can't both claim the same child. You'll want to make some agreements about these sorts of things.

h. **Work on project or business.** If you work together on a onetime project (like building a sailboat or restoring an antique auto) you could define your relationship to it in this agreement (see section E below), but for activities that are more like an ongoing business, you should *definitely* make a separate partnership agreement. When people live together and work on a business without a partnership agreement, it can require a court action to prove an implied contract to gain an equity interest in the business. See Nolo's *The Partnership Book.*

Combinations. Some situations require careful coordination of the options you choose. For example, where a couple owns separate estates and also want to create a joint estate, they'll need to carefully think about distinguishing between joint and separate income, earned income and income from assets, and protecting the joint estate from debts incurred to benefit a separate business or asset.

If you feel uncertain how to accomplish your goals or want to make sure your agreement is being done correctly, talk to a family law attorney (chapter 3B) to get some advice and discuss your options.

2. Things that can't be done

There are things you can't control in a contract, in particular almost anything to do with federal laws, such as federal tax returns, Social Security, appointing beneficiaries under some kinds of retirement accounts and investment funds, and so on. States will always retain the final word on child custody and support.

3. Tax issues—caution!

It's not as if financial issues aren't already complicated enough, but tax laws are another can of worms. Do not design your financial agreement without first getting advice and input from a good tax accountant. For example: shared earnings are taxed first to the earner, then possibly taxed again to the recipient. Financial support in exchange for services requires full treatment as wages. Deposits in a joint account can give rise to imputations of taxable gifts or income where one puts in more than the other. Transfers of property can be a taxable gift and transfers of real property can trigger a reassessment for property tax purposes. One partner might be able to claim exemptions for the other partner or partner's children if they are members of his/her household and receive more than 50% of their support from the claimant. Ask about estate and gift tax consequences for jointly held property. Go over your goals with the tax accountant and see if you can find a way to accomplish them that is relatively painless from a tax point of view. Shop around for a tax accountant who is not just an extension of the IRS; one who is practical and inventive about doing things without arousing attention.

From a tax point of view, the safest thing is to keep separate bank accounts, avoid commingling funds, and make an agreement stating that there is no intention to pool earnings or other income or gifts or inheritances and neither has interest in future earnings of the other from whatever source. Of course, taxes and money aren't the only consideration, but it is something to think about.

C. How committed are you?

The rest of this chapter is most suitable for couples who are interested in a long-term committed relationship because our basic Couples Contract is optimized for people who hope to be together forever, or at least indefinitely.

We understand you might be taking things a day at a time and, even if those days pile up into years, you might not be comfortable with a lot of focus on commitment or long-range planning. The less committed you are, or the more short-term your view, the more we believe you should make your contracts with the help of Nolo's excellent book, *Living Together*, which takes an entire book to cover a far broader range of issues and clauses for unmarried couples than we can cover in this one chapter. But, there is one part of the basic agreement that you should definitely keep in any contract you write—section 9 is extremely important, as it guarantees that no matter what happens, you'll never end up in court. This, alone, is worth the little effort it will take.

Everyone can benefit from continuing on with us, but from this point to the end of the chapter, we are primarily addressing issues we think are common to unmarried couples who expect to be together for the long haul.

Unmarried together forever. Some people like the feeling of waking up every morning and knowing they are together because they want to be, not because they contracted for a life term. Some just don't feel the need to make it official, or to involve the church or state in their personal lives. Some are together because they just are: never thought about it, don't want to think about it. Some are not married because they are still married to someone else and haven't gotten a divorce yet. There must be a host of other reasons, but one thing you all have in common is that you expect to be together indefinitely.

To the extent that you care about each other, you will want to protect one another with the kinds of agreements and documents we described in section A above: durable powers of attorney for health and financial matters, wills, and an agreement that spells out for relatives and others who owns what. Be sure to review the designated beneficiaries on any retirement plans, investment accounts or insurance policies. And, you surely will want to get the advantages of our basic Couples Contract (chapter 2). In the next section, we show you how to tailor the basic Couples Contract for your needs.

Still married to someone else. If you are living together while one of you is still married to someone else, you are in a dangerous situation until the marriage is legally resolved by either a divorce or legal separation. The old relationship is a legal threat hanging over your heads, even if you haven't seen or heard from the old spouse for ages. If you mix your incomes and assets, the old spouse or a creditor for common necessities could show up some day and make a claim which, even if you fend it off, could involve you in an expensive and tiresome squabble.

Get advice. The reasons for staying married while living with someone else vary widely—reluctance to deal with it, reliance on marital benefits, or a spouse who is afflicted with Alzheimer's. Whatever the reason, you could conceivably fall into a thicket of legal tangles, so you should definitely get some legal advice from a family law attorney on your specific situation before you enter into any sort of legal agreement to live together.

D. Changes to the basic agreement

The basic Couples Contract (chapter 2) is optimized for couples who are in a long-term relationship. Its goals are to (1) reinforce your commitment to each other, (2) plant ideas that might help resolve relationship issues in the future, and (3) keep your relationship forever out of court. While you're at it, you can make some financial agreements (section E below).

Being an unmarried couple, you need to make a few changes to the basic agreement and think carefully about the commitments in section 2.

Section 2. Commitments. The law in most states imposes on married people the highest standard of care in dealing with one another, called a *fiduciary* duty, which is pretty much as described in section 2 of the basic Couples Contract. Unmarried couples are presumed to be dealing with each other at arm's length, just like any other adults doing business. However, the law sometimes implies a *confidential* relationship when one person has gained the confidence of the other and claims to be acting in the other's best interest, in which case a *fiduciary* duty is imposed. This can also happen where one person has control of another's property, at least as to the property being controlled. The problem with implied fiduciary duty is that it is not presumed, so if there is a dispute, circumstances giving rise to the fiduciary duty must be proved in court.

Because the Couples Contract is about commitment to a lasting relationship, and because most committed couples are at least arguably in a confidential relationship, we suggest that you leave this clause as written and clearly state that you are taking the high road and commit to a high duty toward each other.

Section 3. Effective date and duration. Replace with the following:

3. Effective date and duration of agreement

This agreement will become effective once it has been signed by both parties and will terminate upon the marriage or cohabitation of one party with a third person, or upon the marriage of the parties to each other, or __ days after the written notice by one party to the other that our relationship and our agreement is being ended, unless we begin counseling during that period of time. During counseling, this period of __ days will be suspended, and will begin again if one party gives written notice to the other and to the counselor(s) that counseling is terminated and the separation is final.

The termination will not be retroactive, so all property and debts defined as joint or separate by this agreement will remain joint or separate, unless specified otherwise elsewhere in this agreement. However, any provisions of this agreement that last for a specific period of time will not be terminated by this notice. Any provisions of this agreement that begin when we separate will begin then.

Section 6. Money and property. Discussed in section E below.

Section 7. Disclosure. If you tailor your financial relationships, you *must* do financial disclosure and use the disclosure clause in chapter 5F. But, we urge you to do disclosure even if not absolutely required as this would be safer for your agreement and better for your relationship.

E.   Tailoring your financial relationships

Tailoring financial relationships means thinking about how to manage your income and expenses, who pays which debts, and who owns which assets. This is done in the context of your separate personalities, your relationship, and your situation in life. Be sure to review *What can be done* in section B1 above.

Caution! Do not make a financial agreement without advice from a tax accountant. Almost every feature could have potential tax consequences which you should be aware of before you decide what to do. See section B3 above.

Caution! Don't mention sex. Not that you were going to, but don't. Any clause or portion of your agreement in which sex is a basis cannot be enforced and it can threaten your entire agreement if it is seen as a central feature. Nothing about sex is enforceable, so best to not mention it *directly*. In all but a few states (Deleware, Illinois, Georgia), an agreement to live together, share property and have children will be seen as an agreement for a committed relationship and therefore enforceable. To read more about enforceability of cohabitation agreements, look in the Legal Briefs folder on the companion CD.

Advice. Unless your situation is simple and the financial clauses obvious you should do your homework here then review your agreement with an experienced family law attorney (see chapter 3B) to review your agreement or get some ideas and options for how to deal with your particular situation. This is especially true if you aren't sure how to go about tailoring your agreement.

How to do it. Add financial clauses under section 6 of the basic Couples Contract, but first label this clause "A" and delete the words "marital and," so it reads like this:

6.   Money, property and financial matters

A.   Except as modified by this agreement, we agree that all of our mutual rights and obligations with respect to our financial affairs, including our income, debts, and property, will be governed by the laws of _____, no matter where we might live in the future.

Each additional clause you add will be labeled B, C, D, etc., in order, depending on which ones and how many you use.

Explanations. After each sample clause we also show a sample explanation that you will use in the Explanation of Agreement document (chapter 8A).

Schedules and exhibits. Whenever you are dealing with more than a few items of property in any clause, rather than list them all in your agreement, you can attach lists at the back of the agreement and label them Schedules 3 and 4 (as in the first example below). The particular number will depend on whatever has come before it in your agreement. In our example, Schedules 1 and 2 are the financial disclosures of the two parties and Exhibit A is always the Nolo Supplementary Family Arbitration Rules.

Disclosure. Don't forget: you *must* do financial disclosure and use the disclosure clause shown in chapter 5F.

Example clauses

Our goal in this section is to illustrate some reasonable solutions for common situations faced by committed unmarried couples. In addition to the situations and clauses below, you should also review chapter 5D, as there could be some ideas there you can adapt.

1. Keeping everything separate

While it might not be emotionally satisfying for couples who see themselves as lifetime partners, this arrangement is cleanest from a tax point of view, and it is highly recommended if one partner is in debt or in a risky business, or where a partner is still married to someone else. It assumes that the parties have their own sources of income so that one is not financially dependent on the other.

Comments

When keeping things separate, always keep the separation in mind and be cautious about departures from your plan. For example, if you open joint accounts, or sign loan or credit applications together, or use each other's assets or income on any application, then those accounts or purchases will not be clearly separate. A pattern of such intermingling can confuse and undermine your plan to keep your financial affairs separate.

Agreement for Example 1

B.   Separate assets. The separate assets and debts of Chris, listed on Schedule 3, and the separate assets and debts of Jamie, listed on Schedule 4, are and will remain their own separate assets and debts, including all profits and appreciation flowing from those assets.

C.   Income and acquisitions are separate. We agree that, unless stated otherwise in this agreement, all income, from whatever source, as well as all acquisitions made with that income, and all gifts or inheritances, will be the separate property of the person who earns or receives it. Neither party will acquire any interest in the separate income or assets of the other party and the separate property of one cannot be transferred to the other unless done in writing.

D.   Separate debts and accounts. We will each maintain separate accounts for all financial activities, such as banking, investing, retirement funds, credit cards, and the like.

Chris will be responsible for all debts incurred by Chris or in the operation of or for the benefit of Chris's separate assets and Chris will indemnify, defend and hold Jamie harmless from any action to collect such debts from joint assets or Jamie's separate property, including paying any costs and attorney fees in connection with such an action.

Jamie will be responsible for all debts incurred by Jamie or in the operation of or for the benefit of Jamie's separate assets and Jamie will indemnify, defend and hold Chris harmless from any action to collect such debts from joint assets or Chris's separate property, including paying any costs and attorney fees in connection with such an action.

E.   Joint accounts. From time to time we might maintain a joint checking or savings account into which we will make equal deposits sufficient to cover our ordinary household expenses for accommodation, food, entertainment, services, utilities, cleaning supplies and the like. Our joint account can also be used to buy property we have agreed to own together, in which case the details of our joint ownership will be put in writing or in the title document to the property.

F.   Division on termination. If this agreement should terminate, as defined in section 3 above, we will each be entitled to immediate possession of our separate property. If, at that time, we co-own any personal property, it will be immediately divided by mutual agreement and, if we cannot agree on how to divide it, we will (insert here one of the ten ways to divide property from Appendix A10).

Explanation for example 1

We agree that everything owned or owed by each of us are separate including all increases or profits from our separate property. All income from any source and all acquisitions made with that income will be the separate property of the person who

2. Keeping everything separate, but . . .

Here are two variations for the "keep everything separate" agreement above, that can be used if you decide to purchase a major item such as a home together, or do a significant joint project together.

How to. You can add these clauses to the above agreement as section 6G or use them both as 6G and 6H. You can also add agreements like these at some later time by modifying your Couples Contract as described in chapter 9G, using the language below in the modification template.

Optional. In either of these situations, you might want to provide for life insurance as a safety net in case one of the partners dies.

a. Joint purchase of real estate or other titled asset

This variation is used for buying titled property, which is typically purchased on time, like a car or, in this example, a home or other real estate.

Comments

Personal loans. If you want to own property together, or engage in a project together, but one partner can't come up with money, the other partner can lend the money. If this happens, be sure to draw up a promissory note detailing the terms of the loan. You can find a promissory note form in stationery stores; call around.

Buying into an existing home. This can be done either with a single payment or buying in a little at a time and acquiring a certain ownership interest with each payment. This all needs to be carefully defined, as well as how routine maintenance, repairs, taxes and insurance will be paid at each stage, and what happens if the agreement is ever terminated. You might need a lawyer's help to draw up this kind of agreement. Contact a lawyer who specializes in real estate transactions.

Buy and fix up. Sometimes one partner will buy the home and the other will contribute sweat equity to fix it up. If this happens, you need to tailor a different agreement to explain how your deal is going to work. You can adapt some ideas from the example below.

b. Joint project

Agreements to participate in a large onetime project, like buying and fixing up a home for resale, can be made separately at any time, but if you happen to be planning one when you make your Couples Contract, you could do it like this. Label this section according to where it appears in the rest of your agreement.

earns or receives it. Neither of us will acquire any interest in the property of the other and the separate property of one cannot be transferred to the other except in writing. We will maintain separate accounts, be responsible for our own debts, and each will protect the other party from any action to collect the debts of one from the other. We will maintain a joint account and each will deposit equal sums into it sufficient to cover our ordinary expenses or to buy property we have agreed to own together. In the event our agreement is terminated, we will each be entitled to immediate possession of our separate property. Any co-owned property will be divided by mutual agreement or, if we cannot agree, then we will divide it by (briefly describe method chosen).

Agreement for example 2a

G. Joint purchase of real estate

1. We agree to jointly purchase the real property at (address),

☐ which we will own equally and take title as (joint tenants/tenants in common)

☐ taking title as tenants in common, which Chris will own __% and Jamie will own __%.

2. We will share all costs of ownership, including the down payment, closing costs, mortgage payments, taxes, insurance, repairs and routine maintenance (equally/according to our percentage of ownership in the property). If one of us pays all or part of the other's share of the expenses, the payer will be entitled to reimbursement plus _ % annual interest for amounts that can be documented.

3. Capital improvements will be made only by mutual consent to the nature, extent and cost of such improvements, and costs will be shared (equally/according to our percentage of ownership in the property).

4. Upon termination of this agreement as provided in section 4 above, one of the following will happen:

(a) We can agree that one of us will assume sole ownership on terms and conditions to be mutually agreed upon at that time;

(b) If neither of us wants to assume sole ownership, or if we can't agree on terms for one of us to buy the other's interest, the property will be listed with a licensed real estate broker within __ days. Net proceeds from sale, if any, will be divided between us (equally/according to percentage of ownership in the property). "Net proceeds from sale" means the total amount received less sales commissions, costs incident to the sale, and amounts paid to discharge outstanding mortgages, liens, encumbrances, or costs defined in G2 above.

(Explanation on next page)

Explanation for example 2(a)

We agree to go in together to purchase (describe), which we will own (say how). We will share all costs (say how). If one of us pays any part of the other's share, the person paying will be entitled to reimbursement plus __% annual interest. Capital improvements will be made only by mutual consent and costs will be shared (say how). In the event of termination of this agreement, then either one of us will assume sole ownership on terms that will be decided at that time, or the property will be listed for sale within __ days and net proceeds from sale will be divided between us (say how).

Agreement for example 2(b)

G. Joint project

1. We agree to join together to build an Acme Firefox XG airplane
    - ☐ which we will own equally
    - ☐ which Chris will own __% and Jamie will own __%

2. ☐ We will each contribute (amount/amount per month)
    - ☐ Chris will contribute (amount/amount per month) and Jamie will contribute (amount/amount per month)

for the purchase of necessary parts, supplies, tools, and work space overhead. These funds will be kept in one or more joint accounts that will be used solely for this project and both of our signatures will be required to withdraw funds from these accounts. If one party pays all or part of the other party's share of the expenses, careful records must be kept as such payments will be entitled to reimbursement plus _ % annual interest.

3. We will each work diligently on this project, which means Chris will work at least __ hours per month and Jamie will work at least __ hours per month on the project, and we will each keep a record on the site of all hours worked.

4. Should either of us die while we are still joint owners of the project, the survivor will become sole owner.

5. Should either of us wish to end his/her participation in this project, then within __ days of giving written notice of intention to withdraw, one of the following will happen:

    (a) One of us will assume sole ownership on terms and conditions to be mutually agreed at that time.

(b) If neither of us wants to assume sole ownership, or if we are not able to agree on terms, the project will be liquidated and sold and net proceeds after paying all related debts and obligations will be distributed between us according to our percentage of ownership in the project.

(c) For purposes of this buy-out clause, "the project" means all money in the joint project accounts and all materials, tools, and supplies contributed to or purchased for the benefit of the project.

(d) Withdrawal from the project will not imply termination of the rest of our agreement, but if our agreement is terminated as defined in section 3 above, the project must also be terminated and divided as specified in this clause unless we make a new written agreement to continue.

Explanation for example 2(b)

We are going to build an airplane together which we will own (say how). We will each contribute (describe) into a joint account, requiring both of our signatures on any transaction, that will be used only to pay for all expenses incurred in the project. If one of us pays any part of the other's share, careful records must be kept and that person will be entitled to reimbursement plus __% interest. Chris will work at least __ hours per month on the project and Jamie will work at least __ hours per month. Should either of us die, the other becomes sole owner of the project. If one of us wants to withdraw from the project, then within __ days of written notice being given, one of the following will happen: (a) one of us will assume sole ownership on terms to be agreed at that time; (b) the project will be liquidated and net proceeds after paying all debts will be divided between us according to our share of ownership in the project. Withdrawal from the project will not imply the termination of the rest of our agreement, but if our agreement should be terminated, the project must also be terminated unless we make a new written agreement to continue.

3. Share income and acquired assets

In this variation, the couple acts more like a traditional family and decides to pool their energies and resources. The first clause itemizes assets and debts that are to be kept separate, if any, and the second clause protects the joint estate from debts incurred to benefit anyone's separate estate. However, you could decide to convert all assets to co-ownership, and do away with separate property and debts altogether. Pooling has the potential for serious tax disadvantages, so do not make this kind of agreement without the advice and input of a good tax accountant.

Caution! Support and transfers of money or assets are potentially taxable events (section B3 above). One wonders how the IRS will hear about money used to support another person or another person's child, but you have to be aware there is a potential problem. See a tax accountant before making this kind of agreement; preferably one who does not seem to be a spokesperson for the IRS.

a. Pooled income and assets, no support

This agreement pools income and assets but does not require that one party support the other.

Note. Clause B refers to Schedules 3 and 4, which is because Schedules 1 and 2 would be for the disclosures of Chris and Jamie (chapter 5F).

b. Adding support for a partner

As an addition to the agreement described above, one partner can agree to support the other, which is especially suitable where one is financially dependent on the other or has sacrificed a job or education in order to be together. Support for a child of the two of you is already defined by state law, but if one of you has a child by another relationship, you might want to provide for support of the child. For either support of a mate or a mate's child, you need to decide if support will continue after the agreement terminates, or after one partner dies, and for how long, if at all.

Agreement for example 3(a)

B. Separate assets. The separate assets and debts of Chris, listed on Schedule 3, and the separate assets and debts of Jamie, listed on Schedule 4, are and will remain their own separate assets and debts, including all profits and appreciation flowing from those assets.

Any gifts or inheritances received by either of us will also be the separate property of the recipient. Neither of us will acquire any interest in the other's separate property except by means of a written document.

C. Separate debts

Chris will be responsible for all debts incurred by Chris or for the benefit of Chris's separate assets and Chris will indemnify, defend and hold Jamie harmless from any action to collect such debts from joint assets or Jamie's separate property, including paying any costs and attorney fees in connection with such an action.

Jamie will be responsible for all debts incurred by Jamie or for the benefit of Jamie's separate assets and Jamie will indemnify, defend and hold Chris harmless from any action to collect such debts from joint assets or Chris's separate property, including paying any costs and attorney fees in connection with such an action.

D. Shared earnings and assets

1.   We agree to combine our efforts and earnings and share equally any assets accumulated through our individual or combined efforts. All income earned or assets acquired by the efforts of either or both of us, will be owned equally as (joint tenants/tenants in common) and will be deposited to joint accounts to which we both have access and/or held in joint title (with right of survivorship).

2.   We will have equal rights of management and control of joint funds and assets, which can be used by either of us to acquire assets on behalf of both of us, for the personal expenses of either or both of us. Neither of us may use joint funds, or funds we have agreed to pool, for the benefit of his/her own separate estate without written consent of the other, and any funds so used without written consent must be reimbursed to our joint account with __% interest.

3.   The contribution of each of us will be deemed to be equal to the contribution of the other regardless of the actual amounts contributed.

E. Support. Other than the obligation to share our earnings, neither of us will be obligated to contribute to the support of the other (or the other's children, if any) during the relationship or after termination of this agreement.

F. Taxes. Each of us will file an individual income tax return reporting his or her own income. Taxes assessed on income pooled under this agreement will be a joint expense payable from our joint account. Taxes assessed on unearned income from separate sources will be the sole obligation of that person and payable from that person's separate income.

G. Division of property. In the event of termination of this agreement, as provided in section 4 above, all liquid assets will be divided equally in kind and non-liquid assets will be divided by mutual agreement so that each receives equal value. If we cannot agree on the division of non-liquid assets, we will (insert here one of the ten ways to divide property from Appendix A).

Explanation for example 3(a)

All assets and debts listed by Chris and Jamie on Schedules 3 and 4, respectively, are their separate property and responsibility. All profits and increases flowing from those separate assets will also be (say what happens). Any gifts or inheritances received by either of us will also be the separate property of the recipient. No interest in our separate property can be transferred to the other except in writing. We are each responsible for all debts incurred in the ownership or operation of our separate property and each will protect the other party from any action to collect the debts of one from the other. From now on, all income and assets accumulated through our individual or combined efforts will be shared (say how) and will be held in joint title or in joint accounts to which we both have full access (requiring both of our signatures). We will have equal rights to manage and control our joint assets, but neither of us can use joint funds for the benefit of our separate property without the other's written consent, and any such funds so used will be reimbursed to the joint account with __% interest. Other than this, neither of us is obligated to support the other either during our relationship or afterward. Taxes due to our joint income will be a joint expense, but taxes flowing from separate property will be the separate expense of the owner of the property. In the event of termination of this agreement, we will divide all liquid joint assets equally in kind and non-liquid joint assets will be divided by mutual agreement or (describe the other method selected).

Agreement for example 3(b)

E. Support

[Optional: Chris will use her best efforts to generate income sufficient to provide a mutually acceptable standard of living. Jamie will render services as companion, housekeeper and cook and assume responsibility for related household tasks.]
Chris will provide all of Jamie's financial support at the same standard of living at which Chris supports herself. This support obligation will begin on the effective date of this agreement and continue until the first to occur of the following: (1) (date);

(2) termination of this agreement as provided in section 3 above; (3) the death of (Chris/Jamie/Chris or Jamie); or (4) the marriage or cohabitation of Jamie with a third person. Each party waives and disclaims any right to support from the other after the support obligation ends as defined in this agreement.

Explanation

Chris agrees to support Jamie at Chris' own standard of living and Jamie will act as Chris' companion, housekeeper and cook. Support will start when this agreement becomes effective and last until the date or conditions specified in the agreement occur, after which neither of us will be obligated to support the other.

Variation to add child support

E. Support

1. Support for Jamie. [as in the example above]

2. Support of child of another relationship. Chris will provide for the ordinary living expenses, medical and dental care, and education for (name each child and state age), who is/are the child(ren) of Jamie and another person. This support obligation shall continue as to each child named until the child reaches the age of majority,

☐ notwithstanding the termination of this agreement for any reason.

☐ or termination of the obligation to support Jamie as defined in this agreement, whichever occurs first.

Explanation for example 3(b)

[Start with the explanation above, then add the following.]

Chris will support (name and age of each child), who is/are the child(ren) of Jamie and another person. This support obligation will last for each child until (the child reaches majority/termination of Chris' obligation to support Jamie).

F. Laws for unmarried couples

This section discusses laws for couples who live together. States are very different: some try to provide a degree of protection for everyone, while a few are relatively antagonistic toward unmarried relationships. It is essential for you to learn about the laws of your state (see chapter 4G) and stay alert, as laws in this area are subject to change. Before you move to another state, be sure to become familiar with those laws, too, as they might be very different from what you are used to.

1. Oral and implied agreements

A contract can be either expressly stated (orally or in writing) or implied from conduct. This means that careless or generous behavior could later be interpreted as an implied agreement—an excellent reason to write things down, to make sure you don't end up in a squabble some day about something that might or might not have been intended. In the famous legal battle of Lee Marvin and Michele Triola, the couple lived together for about seven years then split up. Michele sued, claiming she and Marvin had agreed orally or by implication to share all earnings and assets. She argued that she gave up a singing career to become his house-keeper, cook and companion, and that it would be unfair for Marvin to keep all assets acquired during their relationship. The California Supreme Court agreed[2] and held that principles of oral and implied contracts apply to unmarried couples just as they would to anyone else. Triola's attorney coined the misleading but popular phrase, "palimony," to refer to a court award of property or support to an unmarried cohabitant based on an implied contract. Not every state has adopted the Marvin approach, but courts in many states will in some circumstances protect an unmarried cohabitant's expectations of property ownership, even though the property is held in the name of the other cohabitant. You might want to find out how this works in your home state (see chapter 4G).

2. Dealings are presumed to be at arm's length

Married couples in most states have a *confidential* relationship, which gives rise to a *fiduciary* duty—a very high standard of fairness and openness in dealing with one another. But unmarried couples, no matter how long together, are treated as strangers and are presumed to be dealing at arm's length where one need not be open and forthcoming with the other, so long as there is no outright fraud.

---

[2] *Marvin vs. Marvin* (1976) 18 Cal. 3d 660, 557 P.2d 106.

In most states, a *confidential* relationship (and the fiduciary duty) can arise when one mate gains the confidence of the other and purports to act in the other's best interests, say by undertaking to manage the mate's financial affairs or taking control of the other's property. Thus, most intimate couples would easily qualify; but the problem is that the burden is on the person claiming unfair treatment to prove the circumstances that required a fiduciary duty.

How much better, then, for any loving couple to make it clear in their Couples Contract that they will always deal with each other under the highest standards.

3. Duty of support

Absent a written agreement, there is no duty for unmarried mates to support each other in the present or in the future. However, as established in the *Marvin* case above, some states will imply an agreement for support or to share income from circumstances or conduct of the parties; so, here again, it is very important to have a written agreement that makes it clear whether or not a support obligation exists.

4. Property rights

When a couple has been living together, many states will apply general contract law and principles of equity to decide any legal issues that may arise. This means the ownership of all acquired property is ambiguous and open to argument. Moral of the story: if you are not married it is *very* important to have a written agreement as to who owns what, who pays which debts, and other financial matters. Oral agreements and understandings are better than nothing, but just barely, as they can be difficult to prove. Clear written agreements prevent arguments.

5. Joint accounts and owning property together

It is often convenient to have a joint account for paying household expenses, but there is some risk involved when you do that. One of you needs to be very good at balancing the statement every month to make sure you can cover your checks. Either of you can use all the money in the account at any time and you are both responsible for any overdrafts and charges. If this is a concern, you can arrange the account so that both signatures are required for withdrawals and checks.

Implied agreement? As in the *Marvin* case above, an agreement to share earnings can be oral or implied from conduct, and a joint account could be one piece of evidence to show such an agreement. So, if you open a joint account or get credit together, it would be better to have a written agreement making it clear whether there is an agreement to share income or support one another.

Taxes? If one person regularly puts more money into a joint account than the other, the difference can be treated by the IRS as income or a gift to the person who put in less.[3] It might seem unlikely that they would ever catch on, but if they did, the rule could be applied and back taxes and penalties assessed. It's possible.

Sharing property. If you decide to buy a house or other large asset with your partner, you should have a written agreement about how you will deal with the down payment and all costs of ownership and, especially, how you will deal with the situation when one of you no longer wants to own the property. At least make sure the title and loan documents accurately reflect your ownership interest.

If you separate, you should immediately close all joint bank and credit accounts.

6. Who owes the debts?

Generally, unmarried mates are not responsible for each other's debts. However, if you co-sign a loan, open a joint bank account or sign a credit agreement with your partner, you are responsible for those accounts. Our advice: unless you have a written agreement, keep your finances separate.

7. Having children together

No one ever doubts who a child's mother is, but with fathers it's not always so easy. By ancient legal tradition (begun centuries before DNA tracing) if a married woman has a child, it is presumed to be her husband's and it takes powerful evidence to overcome this presumption. It does not apply to unmarried parents and the presumptions that do apply are weaker. For children born to an unmarried mother, the paternity is an open question. *Paternity* simply means "fatherhood." Because so many rights and responsibilities flow from the parent-child relationship, it is important for unmarried partners to clearly establish the paternity of any children born during their cohabitation.

The easiest way to establish legal paternity is to fill out a Declaration of Paternity at the hospital when the child is born. If you didn't do this at the hospital, you can get the forms from the district attorney's office. A man who fills out this form is giving up some of his rights to DNA testing and making it easier for child support to be collected from him. Don't sign it if you are not sure.

---

[3] Internal Revenue Code § 61(a); Treasury Regulation § 1.61-2(a), (d); *Lucas v. Earl* (1930) 281 U.S. 111

Checking Your Credit

When people live together for a long time, or share credit cards or bank accounts, their credit can get mixed up so that one partner's bad credit can sometimes be attributed to the other. To check this, you can request a copy of your own credit report and check it for errors or outdated information. There are three major credit bureaus that keep national credit records:

- Equifax   (800) 685-1111   www.equifax.com
- Experian   (888) 397-3742   www.experian.com
- Trans Union   (800) 888-4213   www.transunion.com

You are now entitled to one free credit report every year from each of these major credit bureaus. You can contact each bureau individually or apply to all three at once at www.annualcreditreport.com. Either way, you definitely want your report from all three credit bureaus, as their files are not always the same and correcting your records at one organization will not correct them at the other two. If you find an error or outdated information, contact the bureau in writing. They are required by law to investigate and correct errors, so be prepared to provide whatever records you have to prove that there's an error.

On the other hand, signing this form does give the father legal rights to request custody, contest an adoption and establish inheritance rights. Like the decision of whether or not to be legally married, signing this form has legal advantages and disadvantages and should be taken very seriously.

8. Can I take my partner's name?

The rules for how to change your name legally will vary from one state to another, but speaking generally, people over the age of eighteen can use any first, last and middle names they like, so long as they are not doing it to cheat anyone. Check the laws of your own state about this.

9. Medical emergencies

In case of accident, illness or advanced age, who do you want to step in and take care of you? What if you are incapacitated and can't speak for yourself? Without a written document, an unmarried partner has no right to order medical treatment and cannot take charge, even if you have been living together for years, so medical authorities will be forced to turn to parents, adult children or siblings to make medical decisions. In fact, an unmarried partner might even have trouble visiting in a hospital. People sometimes become estranged from relatives, or love them a lot yet still have a higher degree of closeness and trust with someone who is not a relative. You don't want your mate, family and friends to end up fighting over what should be done. Fortunately, there's an easy way to avoid confusion and conflict when minutes are precious. All you have to do is sign a simple but vitally important document called a Health Care Directive. It has two parts:

(1) A Power of Attorney for Health Care, which allows you to name one or more people who can make health care decisions if you are not able to, including the decision to withhold or withdraw life-prolonging procedures.

(2) Instructions for Health Care, which states in advance your wishes regarding how you want to be cared for if you are not able to make decisions yourself, including whether to use life-prolonging procedures.

These are simple forms you can easily do yourself, but each state has their own slightly different version. To find one for your state, ask at a hospital, large clinic, or your doctor's office, or go on the Internet and search under "Health Care Directive" (in quotes) plus the name of your state.

There's one more step you should take to avoid confusion and conflict: after you finish those documents, sit down with your spouse, relatives, and closest friends and show them the documents, give them a copy, and discuss your ideas for how you'd like to be treated if anything happens. This way, everyone will know what you wanted, whether the document can be found or not.

Visiting. The right to visit a patient in the hospital is another right that comes along with marriage. As hurtful as it might be, if you're not married, the person you have lived with for many years might not be allowed to visit you in the hospital. A health care directive will confer these rights on the person of your choice.

After death. The "next of kin" has the right to decide what happens to a person's remains after death. This includes making decisions about organ donation or other anatomical gifts, as well as deciding where the person will be buried and making other funeral arrangements. These rights can also be given to someone else as part of your Health Care Directive.

10. Health insurance

Health insurance is a contractual benefit, which means that each policy has its own terms and conditions. To determine if your policy will cover your partner, contact the plan administrator. Increasingly companies are allowing unmarried partners to participate in health care plans. But beware! Even if you pay the premiums but are not legally married, coverage can be denied if the policy's terms require that a valid marriage exist before extending coverage.

11. Family Leave Act

Employers with 50 or more employees are required to grant leaves of absence of up to four months to employees who have been with the company for at least one year and who need to take time off to care for a new baby, or an ill parent, spouse or child. Unmarried partners have no right to leave to care for an ill mate unless you happen to have an enlightened employer who allows leave for a "significant other." When the employee returns from leave under the Act, the same or a comparable job must be available. The law also requires that employers let workers on leave continue their health care and retirement benefits, although the employer can insist that the employee on leave pay the entire premium.

12. Social Security and other government benefits

a. Social Security

Let's take Social Security first. This is one area where the rights of married and unmarried couples are very different. And, as this is a federal program, the rules are the same in every state. In short, the rule is that unmarried people get nothing other than what you earn individually. The non-wage earner in your relationship will not be entitled to Social Security benefits based on your earnings. On the other hand, if one of you is receiving Social Security benefits as a widow(er) or a former spouse, they may be reduced or eliminated if you get married. The Social Security laws sometimes favor those who are married during their working years and unmarried when they need to collect benefits.

b. Welfare

Generally, if a parent receives welfare for a child and lives with a partner who is not the child's parent, the welfare will continue so long as the partner does not contribute to the support of either the parent or child. Each welfare office handles cohabitation situations differently, so contact your local office to find out exactly what their guidelines and requirements are so your grant won't be cut off or reduced by living with your partner.

A non-related partner has no duty to contribute to the support of his partner's family. If the mother's grant is reduced or cut off because a non-related partner is living in the house, the mother should seek the help of the nearest Legal Aid office. Look in the white pages of your telephone book for the nearest office.

Welfare laws are in a state of change. Check with your local welfare office or Legal Aid for the most up-to-date information.

c. Other government benefits

The rules concerning medical benefits for old and poor Americans are similar to those for welfare benefits. You can have a live-in partner and still get benefits for you and your children as long as your live-in partner does not contribute to the support of you or your children.

If you are receiving any type of government benefit and plan to begin living with your partner, you should call the local government office of the benefit program and ask what the restrictions and requirements are for live-in partners, so you can comply with their rules and not risk losing or reducing your benefits.

d. Pensions and retirement plans, military and death benefits

Life insurance policies allow the policy owner to name the person who will receive the benefits upon the death of the insured. This is a contract right, and generally can be assigned to anyone you choose, including your unmarried partner. The same is true of defined contribution retirement plans—funds you pay into and accumulate value through investments you direct, like an IRA or 401(k) plan. If you die, the money in your account is paid to the person you designate. If you are not married, you generally can designate any beneficiary you want. If you want these benefits to go to your partner on your death, fill out the paperwork with your employer, insurance company, bank or broker. Most other kinds of retirement plans only pay death benefits to your spouse or dependent children. These include most public and private pension plans that pay benefits based on a formula, rather than on the amount you contributed. Military and other federal government plans won't provide spousal benefits unless you are legally married, which (being federal) does not include members of civil unions or domestic partnerships.

13. Will I inherit from my partner?

States have intestate laws that determine who inherits if a person dies without a will. Under such laws, a person who is not married will inherit nothing, as he or she is not considered an heir. Depending on the survivor's other resources, this can create serious financial difficulty. If you are involved in a living-together relationship and want your partner to inherit from you, make sure you have a valid will or trust naming him or her as a beneficiary. See Nolo's *Will Book* and *Make Your Own Living Trust* at www.nolo.com.

14. Can I get compensation if my partner is killed or injured?

A married person can recover damages for the wrongful death of his or her spouse. However, unmarried people are generally not authorized to bring a wrongful death action. Likewise, a spouse might have rights if his/her partner is negligently injured, but unmarried people do not have these rights—if your mate gets injured or killed through someone's negligence, you can't do anything about it.

Examples

Mickey and Minnie, married for 20 years, were at Disneyland riding Space Mountain when the car flew off the track, killing Minnie. Minnie was Mickey's only means of support. Mickey would be allowed to sue Disney for the wrongful death of Minnie.

Daisy and Donald, who lived together for 20 years, were at Disneyland riding Space Mountain in the same car with Mickey and Minnie. Donald was killed and was Daisy's only means of support. Daisy cannot sue Disney under her state's wrongful death laws because she and Donald were never married.

Likewise, married persons are also able to recover damages for *loss of consortium* when one spouse is injured or killed. *Consortium* encompasses companionship, love, affection, sex—all the comforts that flow from relationship. This is not available to unmarried partners.

15. Taxes

Nonmarital partners are not allowed to file joint income tax returns. Depending on your income level, this may or may not be a disadvantage. Support or other assets transferred between unmarried people could be subject to federal gift tax.[4] Assets inherited by a surviving nonmarital partner are subject to the federal estate tax which is in a state of constant change as to amounts exempted. We think all unmarried couples should see a Certified Financial Planner or tax accountant to get some advice and do some planning.

---

[4] Each person has a federal gift-tax exclusion of $11,000 per year and a $1,000,000 lifetime exemption, which is reduced by the amount of gifts that exceed $11,000 per year.

16. Can a landlord refuse to rent to us?

In most states, landlords are prohibited from discriminating against prospective tenants on the basis of gender or race, and some states include marital status in that mix, but that does not necessarily mean a landlord must rent to people who he/she believes are living in a sinful relationship. The laws on this issue are in flux and states vary widely, so check yours.

17. What if we move?

A few states still make cohabitation illegal for unmarried people and a few refuse to enforce cohabitation agreements on public policy gounds.[5] If you move to another state, have your relationship agreement reviewed by a family law attorney there to find out if it is valid in your new state and discuss options if it is not.

*   *   *

So, there you have it—a brief overview of how unmarried relationships differ legally from marriage, a discussion that applies equally whether the relationship is hetero- or homosexual. For more in-formation, we recommend Nolo's books *Living Together: A Guide for Unmarried Couples* and *A Legal Guide for Lesbian & Gay Couples.*

---

[5] In Delaware and Illinois, contracts based on romantic involvement including sexual favors are unenforceable. Georgia has cases going both ways, so best to get advice there. To read more about enforceability of cohabitation agreements, look in the Legal Briefs folder on the CD.

CHAPTER

8

Two supporting documents

If you use an attorney, the attorney will advise you how things are done in your state. Be sure to tell your attorney that you want your contract to be enforceable in *any* state, in case you move. For people who are doing their own contracts, this chapter and the next detail the steps you must take to make sure your agreement is enforceable. These steps are meant to satisfy checks that were put in place by courts and lawmakers to help prevent abuses. Don't worry; just follow our instructions and you'll be fine. It goes like this:

 Do full financial disclosure if you are tailoring your financial relationships
 Complete the two additional documents in this chapter
☐ Present the final agreement and Explanation to each other (chapter 9B)
☐ Observe the waiting period (chapter 9B)
☐ Have a little (or big or festive) signing ceremony (chapter 9C)

It's all laid out for you here and in the next chapter. If you want to know why we've advised you to take these steps, read section C below.

A. Explanation of Agreement

This document should be prepared and presented to each party along with the final draft of the Couples Contract, at least seven days before it is signed.

This is a bit of bother, since you need to make sure that each significant feature of your agreement is explained in relatively simple terms and explained again in terms of what each party is giving up. Don't worry, we'll help you do it. Here's the template for your Explanation.

Title. Use the words, "Explanation of" followed by whatever title you gave your relationship agreement, then add "between (names)" if your title didn't already include those words.

Governing law. In section C, enter the name of your home state (where at least one party resides permanently when signing your Couples Contract).

Beyond the basic. If you added more terms to your basic contract, check the box in section C and explain each additional feature with language given in chapters where the additional features you used were discussed.

Unmarried couples. In section C, you would replace "during our marriage" with "during the term of our agreement."

Explanation of Relationship Agreement
Between Chris Brown and Jamie Jones

We, Chris Brown and Jamie Jones, give this explanation to each other of the terms and basic effect of our relationship agreement and the rights and obligations that will be given up by each of us if we sign it.

A. We advise each other to consider getting independent legal counsel in connection with the negotiation, drafting and signing of our relationship agreement before signing it.

B. General terms:

    1. The general terms and basic effects of our relationship agreement and are:

        a. To affirm our commitment to a lasting relationship based upon mutual respect, affection and friendship.

        b. To establish principles that will help us resolve personal issues, should any arise, that might threaten to undermine our relationship.

        c. To commit ourselves, in all dealings between us, to mutual respect, openness, honesty and the highest standard of good-faith dealing in all matters, putting each other's interests equal to our own.

        d. To make our relationship agreement effective from (date of signing/date of our marriage) and to remain in effect indefinitely, or until we sign a written agreement to revoke it (unmarried couples add: ",or until the date of termination").

        e. To govern our rights and obligations, wherever we might reside, according to the laws of _____, except as otherwise specified in our agreement.

        f. To waive our right to further disclosure beyond that which is attached to and described in our agreement.

        g. To each waive our right to be represented by independent counsel in the negotiation and preparation of our agreement.

        h. If ever any dispute should arise between us, or under our agreement, that we cannot solve ourselves or with the aid of counselors, we will not take it to court, but instead we will go through mediation and, if mediation fails, we will submit our dispute to binding arbitration.

2. By signing our agreement, we are each giving up the following:

    a. The right to have our contract, or our mutual rights and duties, determined by the laws of any other state in which we might someday reside.

    b. The right to have further financial disclosure beyond that which was given or to claim that what was given was not sufficient.

    c. The right to be represented by an independent attorney in the negotiation, drafting or signing of our agreement. We both understand the wisdom of getting advice from independent counsel, and both had the funds to do so had we wished. We have both had the time and opportunity to ask for as much advice from attorneys or other professionals as we desire.

    d. The right to go to court over any dispute that might arise between us or under our agreement, being required instead to resolve such disputes by mediation or binding arbitration, and the right to have a court choose a mediator for us.

    e. The right to claim that consent to our agreement was not given knowingly or voluntarily.

C. Financial terms, their basic effects, and rights given up:

We are each giving up the right to have our financial affairs governed by the laws of some other state in which we might someday reside. We agree that, during our marriage, wherever we might reside, our financial affairs will be governed according to law.s of
_____, ☐ except as follows:

    A. ...

    B. ...

This document was presented to Chris by Jamie, along with the final draft of our relationship agreement, on _____, 20__.

Date: _____   _____
                            Chris Brown

This document was presented to Jamie by Chris, along with the final draft of our relationship agreement, on _____, 20__.

Date: _____   _____
                            Jamie Jones

B. Waiver of counsel and receipt of Explanation

This document, illustrated below, accomplishes two important purposes. It is a waiver of the right to legal counsel and a declaration that the Explanation and final draft of your agreement were received on a certain date. You'll need one of these documents for each party, to be signed at the same time you sign your Couples Contract. We illustrated only one document here, but the other party must sign one exactly like it, only with the names reversed.

C. But, why?

Some of the steps we ask you to take in this chapter and the next may seem mysterious until you dig into historical abuses and political overreaction and study the cases and statutes that resulted. Here are few words of explanation.

Premarital agreements. Because they were so often abused to produce results that seemed unfair, legislators put up hoops that you must jump through in order to make an enforceable premarital (prenuptial) agreement. This explains the need for (1) full financial disclosure, and (2) the two additional required documents described in this chapter, where the parties must explain to each other in detail the basic effect of the agreement and what rights and benefits are being given up, and state in another document how they really, no kidding, definitely, honest, do not want to retain independent counsel for each party. Oh, well, it's just a little more paperwork.

Marital agreements. Once you're married, the law expects you to look out for each other's best interests—that's the fiduciary duty in action—so if you make an agreement where it looks like one spouse gained an advantage, a judge might presume that undue influence was exerted and refuse to enforce the agreement in that regard (though other parts can remain valid). This presumption can be rebutted, but the burden is on the spouse who gained the advantage. No problem; if you follow the same steps we use to protect the enforceability of a premarital agreement, it will be perfectly clear that the agreement was signed with full knowledge of its meaning and without undue influence.

Living together. Most states impose few legal limits on agreements between unmarried adults, but because most such couples have a close and trusting relationship, it is always possible for one to claim they were in a *confidential* relationship when the agreement was signed and that an unfair advantage was taken. So you, too, will take the extra steps we prescribe to make sure your agreement is not open to attack at some later date.

Protecting your agreement

You need to make sure your Couples Contract is not open to attack if ever things go wrong and what once was love and roses turns to sour grapes. Even if you can't imagine your loved one ever challenging your agreement, you need to protect against possible challenges by other people whose rights might be affected. For example, an agreement to transmute a separately owned house to joint tenancy could conceivably be challenged after death by that person's heirs. So, no matter when you make your agreement or what's in it, here are steps you'll take to make sure your agreement is enforceable and not open to attack.

First, if there was any financial tailoring, you'll do a careful and thorough job on the financial disclosures (chapter 5F) and likewise on the Explanation of Agreement (section A above). Finally, at the time you sign your final agreement, you will also sign a waiver of legal counsel (section B above).

While all this is essential, it is still not enough, because nothing you can write down and sign is certain to convince a judge that there was no undue influence. Judges know that spouses and lovers trust each other and it is quite common for one to sign a document without reading it when asked by the other or under pressure and assurances from the other. So, you need to find some *external* way to demonstrate that a spouse or lover who gives up something understands completely what is being given up and is agreeing to do so without being influenced, only because he/she thinks it is fair.

Signing ceremony. The best way to protect your agreement is to have a signing ceremony with a witness to observe the two of you discussing the agreement in a way that shows that both of you understand the agreement, what is being given up, why it seems fair, and that you are each signing the agreement voluntarily without any influence being exerted by the other. Your witness should be someone reliable—a minister, accountant, lawyer, notary, or other professional would be good—who signs a notarized (or "acknowledged") declaration as to what was said and done. How to do the signing, and how to make it a lovely event if you want to, is described more fully in chapter 9C. An added plus would be to also videotape the signing.

Waiver of Right to Independent Counsel
and Acknowledgment of Receipt of Explanation

I, Chris Brown, hereby declare that I am about to execute a relationship agreement with Jamie Jones. I will refer to us from now on by our first names.

A.   Our relationship agreement was prepared by ☐ Chris ☐ Jamie ☐ both of us working together.

B.   We presented each other with a final draft of our agreement on (date). At that time Jamie advised me, in writing, to seek independent legal counsel before negotiating, drafting or signing our agreement. On that same date, I received from Jamie a copy of the Explanation of Agreement, which I read and understood. I am fully informed of the terms and basic effect of the agreement, as well as the rights and obligations I am giving up by signing it. This was explained to me both orally and in writing in English, and I am proficient in the English language.

C.   I have obtained as much advice, legal and otherwise, as I wish to receive regarding this agreement. I had sufficient funds available to me to retain counsel or other assistance had I wished to do so. I hereby expressly waive my right to be represented by independent legal counsel in the negotiation, drafting or signing of our relationship agreement.

D.   The agreement and this declaration were executed freely and voluntarily, without duress, fraud, or undue influence. I am over the age of 18 and have legal capacity to enter into an agreement.

I declare under penalty of perjury under the laws of the State of _____ that the foregoing is true

This declaration was executed on (date) at (place).

_____

Chris Brown

CHAPTER

9

The final steps

A. Lawyer review?

If you added features to the basic Couples Contract, then now that you have assembled your Couples Contract, Explanation of Agreement, and Waiver of Counsel documents, you are ready for a lawyer review if you want suggestions for improvements or to see if there is anything you might not have thought of. If you want a lawyer (or any other expert) to review your agreement, both of you must clearly understand that you are still looking for input and are open to making changes to get a better agreement.

- If you go for advice or review, take your documents and a copy of this book to the professional you choose (chapter 3B).
- If you are not having a review or your documents, or if they have already been reviewed and are now in final form, it's time for the presentation.

B. Presentation and waiting period

Duplicate originals. You should make at least two copies of every document—one for each of you—and, possibly, a third set for your witness (section C below). While not necessary, you might want to print your relationship agreement on high-quality paper of heavier weight, perhaps even vellum, to give it the feel and appearance it deserves.

All copies should be crisp and clean as you will both sign them later as duplicate originals. This means that you will each end up with a signed original of each document: your Couples Contract with any attachments, the Explanation of Agreement, and the Waiver of Counsel. If you have a witness to the signing (section C below) you will also have a duplicate original of the Witness Declaration.

Presentation means only that at some convenient time and place in your home state, you hand each other the following documents in their final form:

- [ ] The Couples Contract
- [ ] If financial tailoring is involved, your two financial disclosures must be attached to the agreement as Schedules 1 and 2 (chapter 5F)
- [ ] Explanation of Agreement (chapter 8A)

Date and sign. At this time, you each date and sign the Explanation of Agreement. At the bottom of the relationship agreement, you should enter the date you exchange it, but do *not* sign it at this time.

Waiting period. After the presentation, you must wait *at least* seven days before you sign the agreement. This is to make it obvious that you each had time to consider the agreement in its final form, the attached financial disclosures, and the Explanation of Agreement. If either of your financial disclosures includes information that might lead a reasonable person to, for example, order a credit report or ask a professional to review business records or appraisals, you have to wait long enough that it will later appear obvious that a person would have had plenty of time to look into these matters it they wanted to—several weeks or more, depending on what is in the disclosures. Give yourselves plenty of time so you don't have to rush to sign documents before a wedding or any other planned event.

If one or the other of you requests changes to the agreement, prepare the modified agreement, then repeat this presentation step and start the waiting period again.

C.   Signing your agreement and waiver

After the reasonable waiting period described above, you can both sit down together at a convenient time and place and sign duplicate originals of your Couples Contract and the Waiver of Counsel.

Signing ceremony. The best way to make sure your agreement was signed voluntarily with full knowledge of what was in it is to have a bit of a ceremony when you sign it. At a minimum, this means that you will sign in the presence of a reliable witness and make a video and/or audio recording of the two of you discussing what you're agreeing to before you each sign it. The purpose for this signing ceremony is to create *external* evidence that shows you both understood the agreement as well as any advantages that were being given up by signing it, and that signing the agreement was voluntary and without undue influence being exercised by anyone.

Make it an event? You might want to make this into a special occasion, which it truly is. You have accomplished something important together and by your signatures you are making a profound commitment to a lasting relationship. This can be a dress-up event with appetizers, champagne, flowers, candles, family and close friends, and someone to take photos for your album. Let your heart be your guide.

Privacy. To keep your financial affairs to yourselves, you might want to have a private meeting with just you two and the witness where you go over those details, then emerge and read to each other the nicer commitment parts of your agreement, then you and the witness sign documents. Good show.

Skip it? Do not skip the signing ceremony if your agreement adds variations from chapters 5, 6 or 7, or if you are already married when you sign. If you are not already married, and you are only doing the basic agreement in chapter 2, you can, if you wish, simply sign your agreement without the witness, taping or other ceremony and move on to section D below.

How to do it. Of the three ways to preserve evidence that the signers were fully aware and voluntary, the declaration of a witness is essential because a signed and notarized document can be kept indefinitely for future use. A video recording would be the most fun and the most convincing evidence, but you might some day face the problem of finding antique equipment to view whatever you created. Imagine having to go out today to find an 8-millimeter film projector or an 8-inch floppy disk drive or an eight-track tape player. Don't let that stop you from making the video or audio tape, but be sure to get the notarized declaration of a witness above all else.

Any adult can be a witness, but you should choose a mature person who is not a relative of either party. It would be icing on the cake if your witness is someone in a position that implies reliability—a minister, attorney, accountant, etc.

What to say. At the very least, before signing documents, each of you needs to say enough out loud to show the witness—and anyone who watches your video or listens to your audio tape—that you know what the agreement means, what rights you are giving up when you sign it, that you are not being influenced by the other party or anyone else, and that you are signing the agreement voluntarily because you want to and think it is right and fair to do so. Below is a sample script for how this could go. The other party should follow the same script but would, of course, change the names. This script is only a guide: you can use your own words, no need to be formal. If you prefer, you could make a checklist of topics covered in the agreement, and each party could say something about what they understand it to mean or why they want to put it in the agreement. Above all, relax. Don't be worried you'll make a mistake in your ceremony. You are doing something new to show your commitment to each other, and you want to share this with your witness.

Signing Ceremony Script
for Chris Brown

Today, with a full heart and open mind, I am entering into a relationship agreement with Jamie Jones.

[Optional]

I am making this agreement in order to commit myself to a long and lasting relationship based on mutual respect, affection and friendship.

I am committing myself to the highest standard of good faith, openness and honesty in all matters between Jamie and me.

In this agreement, we establish principles and guidelines that can help us resolve personal issues, if any should ever arise, that might threaten to undermine our mutual regard.

[Add any other language you feel suitable to the agreement or the occasion]

I understand that by signing this agreement, I am giving up certain rights.

A.   I am giving up the right to be represented by independent counsel in the negotiation and drafting of our agreement. I am aware that I have the right to have independent counsel represent me, and I had enough time, opportunity and funds available to get as much advice or assistance as I wanted, but, nonetheless, I have chosen not to be represented.

B.   We do not believe that any serious disagreement will ever come between us that we won't be able to resolve, but we also want to make sure our relationship never ends up in court, so we are agreeing that if we ever do have a disagreement that we can't resolve even with help, we are both giving up the right to take our family problem to court. Instead we will use mediation and, if that fails, we will get a final decision through binding arbitration.

[Faith-based option] We have agreed that any conciliator, mediator or arbitrator we use will be a member of (state organization or faith), which means we are giving up the right to choose otherwise qualified professionals who are not members of (organization or faith).

C. I am completely satisfied with the financial disclosure that Jamie gave me and feel that I know all that I want or need to know about our present financial facts. I am giving up the right to ask for any more disclosure before I sign, or to claim that the disclosure I received was not sufficient. We'll continue to be open with each other about our finances in the future, but at this moment I'm satisfied that I know enough to sign this agreement intelligently.

D. Except as modified by our agreement, we are agreeing to have the rights and duties of our relationship governed according to the laws of _____, no matter where we might live in the future, which means I am giving up the right to have my rights governed by the laws of another state we might move to.

    1. [Financial or faith-based explanations added to the basic agreement, taken from the Explanation language given in each chapter]

    2. . . .

E. I understand the terms of this agreement and what I am giving up by signing it. I am not being influenced to sign it by anyone or by any factor other than my own good judgment. I am signing because I think it is fair and in my own best interest to do so and I am giving up the right to claim otherwise in the future. In short, I am signing this agreement freely and voluntarily because I want to.

Signing. When you have each spoken your piece, you each sign two copies (duplicate originals) of your relationship agreement and Waiver of Counsel.

Initial each page. While not required, it is good practice for each party to initial the lower left corner or lower right margin of each page of the agreement and attachments before signing.

Witness. When you have both signed, the witness signs two copies (duplicate originals) of the Witness Declaration, which is illustrated on the next page. After this, more audio or video taping is optional.

Notarization. Some states (notably New Mexico, Louisiana, Minnesota, and New York) require that signatures on prenuptial agreements be notarized (or "acknowledged"), but everyone in all states should have the signatures of both parties and the witness notarized on all documents. Even if your home state does not require notarization, you might some day move to a state that does. You can either arrange to have a notary present at the signing ceremony or right after the ceremony go to a notary's office with your witness and sign the documents there. It is best to actually sign in front of the notary, but it is also possible to sign a second time before the notary or to sign an additional document that the notary will provide acknowledging that the signature on the document is yours.

More witnesses? You can use more than one witness, if you want to; just make a separate Declaration for each of them. If you are doing a faith-based agreement, some religions have their own requirements about the number of witnesses and their qualifications. You can add a statement of their qualifications to paragraph 1, if you like. Ask your clergyperson or religious advisor about this if you want your agreement to be binding under religious law as well as state law.

Guest signatures. This is optional, but if you are having family and friends at your signing, you can invite them to share the occasion by signing a declaration recording their participation. Right after the formal Witness Declaration, we've put an example of a Declaration to Bear Witness so you can see what one might look like; customize it any way you like, as its main purpose isn't legal but to recognize the fact that your community is part of your relationship, too. You could make copies of this group declaration after the ceremony and give one to each of your witnesses.

Duplicate originals. You each get a signed duplicate original of all documents, which you should put in a safe place (section D below). Make two or more copies of each document that you can keep around for reference, but you should each put your copies of the originals in a very safe place.

Declaration of Witness to Signing
of Chris and Jamie's Relationship Agreement

I, the undersigned, declare as follows:

1. I am (name), (age) years old, and a (occupation) in (city, state).

2. I am not related to Chris Brown or Jamie Jones.

3. On (date), at approximately (time), I was personally present at (location, city, state) when Chris Brown and Jamie Jones signed their relationship agreement. I was given a copy of the documents they signed, and I was in a position to hear clearly every word spoken and was paying close attention as they each discussed the contents of their agreement.

4. I clearly heard Chris Brown describe in her own words the terms of the agreement and what she was giving up by signing it. She stated that she understood every word of it and was signing of her own free will, in full understanding of the meaning of the terms, and without being influenced by anyone was signing because she thought it was fair and reasonable and in her own best interest to do so.

5. I clearly heard Jamie Jones describe in his own words the terms of the agreement and what he was giving up by signing it. He stated that he understood every word of it and was signing of his own free will, in full understanding of the meaning of the terms, and without being influenced by anyone was signing because he thought it was fair and reasonable and in his own best interest to do so.

6. It appeared to me, and according to my own best judgment, that both parties understood the meaning of their agreement and what they were gaining and giving up by signing it, and that they were each signing it freely, voluntarily and without undue influence because they thought it was fair and reasonable and in their own best interest to do so.

I declare under penalty of perjury that the foregoing is true and correct.

Dated: _____   _____
                                          (signature of witness)

Declaration to Bear Witness to Signing
of Chris and Jamie's Relationship Agreement

We, the undersigned, solemnly declare:

On (date), at (city, state), we were present to bear witness when Chris Brown and Jamie Jones signed their relationship agreement.

By their agreement, Chris and Jamie committed themselves to a lasting relationship, and promised never to take any dispute between them to court. Chris and Jamie explained to us why they were making this commitment, and that they understood the legal meaning of their agreement and any rights they were giving up. They signed it freely and voluntarily.

As their friends, family, and witnesses, we pledge to support Chris and Jamie in helping them keep the commitments they made to each other today. We specifically promise to help them lovingly and respectfully resolve any issues that might arise between them, and to encourage them to use the methods they agreed today to use in case they encounter matters they cannot resolve by themselves. We will encourage them to live together in a relationship of trust, mutual respect, affection and friendship.

In witness of these promises, we sign this declaration on (date), at (city, state).

_____ _____

_____ _____

_____ _____

_____ _____

_____ _____

_____ _____

_____ _____

D. Store documents safely

Your agreement won't mean much if you can't find it later when you want it. "Later" might mean ten or thirty years in the future. This is one of those important documents that you never want to lose. So, first, you should each make two extra copies of your signed originals. Then, put each set of documents in a 9 x 12 envelope. Keep one set at home where it is easy to get at if you want to review it, and put the signed originals in a very safe place. The ideal place would be a safe deposit box, but that costs a monthly fee forever. Next safest would be a fireproof safe, filing cabinet or document box kept at home and, finally, any other safe and secure place at home. The second set of copies should be put somewhere else, like the home of a relative or friend, just in case your originals are lost or destroyed by accident.

E. Follow through

After you sign your agreement, you both need to do anything you agreed to do and avoid doing anything not consistent with your agreement. You don't want your agreement to say one thing and your actions later to say something else. This is especially important if you are trying to keep income and debts separate.

Transfers. If your agreement calls for you to change separate property into marital property or vice-versa, you will need to actually make the transfers as soon as possible after the agreement becomes effective. If you are not yet married, this means right after your wedding. If you are already married, or don't plan to, it means right after you sign. For real estate, contact a real estate professional or an attorney about what kind of deed to use in your state to accomplish your purpose. Interspousal transfers do not have federal tax consequenes, but a transfer between unmarried people probably will. There could also be property tax consequences if the basis of the property were to change as a result of the transfer. Consult a tax accountant about this.

Set up accounts. In many situations, you will need to set up both separate and joint accounts for holding funds, and perhaps you'll want both joint and separate credit card accounts, too. If you are trying to protect your separate income from your spouse's debts, you will want to close all joint credit card accounts.

Keep separate things separate. If either of you owns separate assets or separate income during marriage and want to keep it that way, it is essential that you keep that property under separate title or in separate accounts.

- Do not mix ("commingle") marital funds with separate funds in any account, no matter how temporary or how convenient it might seem.
- When applying for joint credit, do not list a spouse's separate income or assets on the application and do not use a spouse's separate property as security.
- When applying for separate credit, make sure the application is in one name only and do not list marital assets or income as a basis for the loan.

Wills, estate planning. After you complete your agreement, you might want to look into estate planning tools, such as wills, living trusts, powers of attorney for health care and financial management in case of disability, and so on. Nolo has several fine books and software products to help you with this. Look for them in your local public library or on-line at www.nolo.com.

F. Periodic reviews

Times change, laws change, your circumstances can change and your relationship can change, too. It only makes sense to take your agreement out every few years and see if it still makes sense in the light of the new you. See if you still want exactly what it says, or if maybe you'd like to change anything. If your agreement has any clauses that expire on a certain date or condition, then it would be smart to take a look at the agreement some time before that date or condition is about to happen so you can see if any action needs to be taken. When anything significant happens—children, change in employment, moving to another state, a big raise—this would be a good time to look back over your agreement. Sit down and talk to each other about the agreement in light of changed circumstances, just like you did when you first made your agreement.

If you agree to change anything about your agreement, you'll need to modify your agreement in writing.

G. How to modify your agreement

Your agreement can only be modified in writing, and you will go through exactly the same steps that you did to make your Couples Contract. This means doing disclosure (chapter 5F), the Explanation of Agreement (chapter 8A), presentation and waiting period (chapter 9B), and signing before a witness (chapter 9C). One big difference is that your modification agreement will probably be a lot easier to write, as you only have to write those clauses that are being changed.

A modification agreement would look something like the example that starts on the next page.

1. Circumstances. Briefly summarize whatever it is that has changed that has caused you to want to modify your agreement. It might be some actual factual difference or just that after living together for some time you now have different goals or ideas about how you want to live.

2. Modification. Modification can mean quite a range of possible changes to your original agreement. As illustrated in the example clauses, you can:
- revoke whole clauses (clause 2A in the example modification)
- replace specific clauses with new wording (example 2B)
- add new agreements (example 2C)

or any combination of these. Use whatever it takes to get the effect you want. Remove the check boxes if you work on a typewriter or word processor. If you use only one modification clause, also remove the letter label. If you use more than one modification clause, label each different segment and make sure they are labeled in order.

Make sure that your new contract language is perfectly clear, consistent with the rest of your agreement (otherwise make more changes), and not subject to being interpreted in more than one way. See chapter 3C(2) on writing clauses.

5. Disclosures. If you are not changing any financial relationships, you can get away with using the simple waiver of disclosure illustrated at section 7 in the basic agreement (chapter 2). However, if any financial changes are being made in your modification, you will want to do the full disclosure as illustrated in the language shown here. For how to do the disclosure documents, see chapter 5F.

Notarized signatures. Modifications require the same formalities as original agreements. Many states require that you notarize your signatures so best to sign before a notary in every case.

Modification of Relationship Agreement

On (date), we, Chris and Jamie, entered into a relationship agreement, a copy of which is attached and incorporated by reference. Our circumstances and goals have changed, so that now we wish to make the specific changes set forth below. In all other regards, we intend for our original agreement to continue in full force and effect.

1. Circumstances

The circumstances that have caused us to want to modify our agreement are (describe briefly, just the high points):

2. Modification

    A. ☐ We agree to revoke (clause or section numbers to be revoked)

    B. ☐ We agree to change (clause or section number) of our original agreement to read as follows: (specify)

    C. ☐ We agree to change our original agreement by adding the following new agreements to it: (specify)

3. Construction

If there should be any conflict or inconsistency between the original agreement and this modification, the provisions and intentions of the modification should control in all respects.

4. Representation and drafting

☐ Chris and Jamie drafted this modification together, jointly.

☐ This modification was primarily drafted by ☐ Chris ☐ Jamie

I, Chris, understand that I have the right to be represented by an independent lawyer in the negotiation and preparation of this modification and I have sufficient funds to retain a lawyer for this purpose if I wanted to. Nonetheless, I choose not to be represented. I understand the terms of this agreement and freely and voluntarily choose to sign it without recourse to legal counsel.

I, Jamie, understand that I have the right to be represented by an independent lawyer in the negotiation and preparation of this agreement and I have sufficient funds to retain a lawyer for this purpose if I wanted to. Nonetheless, I choose not to be represented. I understand the terms of this agreement and freely and voluntarily choose to sign it without recourse to legal counsel.

5. Disclosures

Each of us has made a full, fair and reasonable disclosure to the other of annual income, all assets owned and all obligations owed on the date such information was presented.

A list of our marital income, assets and obligations is set forth in Schedule 1, which is attached to and made part of this agreement.

[Optional]
Attached to Schedule 1 is/are the following additional document(s):
☐ our joint federal and/or state tax return for years (years) ☐ other (specify).

A list of Chris's separate income, assets and obligations is set forth in Schedule 2, which is attached to and made part of this agreement.

[Optional]
Attached to Schedule 2 is/are the following additional document(s):
☐ Chris's separate federal and/or state tax return for years (years) ☐ the following appraisals: (name them) ☐ credit report ☐ other (specify).

A list of Jamie's income, assets owned and obligations owed by Jamie is set forth in Schedule 3, which is attached to and made part of this agreement.

[Optional]
Attached to Schedule 3 is/are the following additional document(s):
☐ Jamie's separate federal and/or state tax return for years (years) ☐ the following appraisals: (name them) ☐ credit report ☐ other (specify).]

We each understand that values set forth in Schedules 1, 2 and 3 are approximate values on the date presented, estimated to the best of our ability, but not necessarily exact.

I, Chris, received a copy of Schedules 1 and 3 [and attached documents named above] on (date), and reviewed that information before signing this agreement. I consider this information to be sufficient and waive the right to be given further information.

I, Jamie, received a copy of Schedules 1 and 2 [and attached documents named above] on (date), and reviewed that information before signing this agreement. I consider this information to be sufficient and waive the right to be given further information.

Signatures

We have each read this agreement carefully and are signing it freely, voluntarily, and with full understanding of its meaning after having obtained all the advice we each, individually, feel is appropriate.

This agreement was delivered to Chris by Jamie on (date)

Dated: _____   _____
                                Chris Brown

This agreement was delivered to Jamie by Chris on (date)

Dated: _____   _____
                                Jamie Jones

Attachments

☐ Schedule 1   Chris's financial disclosure
☐ Schedule 2   Jamie's financial disclosure

Originals and copies. Sign duplicate originals and make copies of your modification agreement just as you did with your Couples Contract (section C above).

Store it safely. Store the originals and copies of your modification agreement with the originals and copies of your Couples Contract (section D above).

H. Portability
—taking your agreement to other states

If you move to another state, your agreement will be interpreted by the courts in that state according to their laws. Of course, your agreement has clause 10D stating that it is to be interpreted according to the laws of your home state, and clause 9B says that any dispute that you cannot settle will be decided by a family law attorney from your home state acting as arbitrator. Between these two clauses, your document will probably hold up just as you intended when you signed it. However, to be absolutely certain, if you addeed features to your basic Couples Contract, you should have it reviewed by an experienced family law attorney in your new state. It's the safe thing to do.

APPENDIX

A

Ending smoothly if it has to be over
(How to reduce pain and cost)

This book is about lasting relationships and how to preserve them, but sometimes they can't be saved. Breaking up[1] is almost always painful, but the essential thing is to avoid *unnecessary* pain and cost, much of which can be avoided or minimized if you are careful. It is essential to avoid words and actions that escalate from hurt, fear, and anger to hostility, lawyers, courts, and huge expense. That would be very hard on you, on your kids if you have any, and devastating to your pocketbook. There are ways to go about breaking up that will give you the best chance for a smoother trip through one of life's most difficult passages. This is an exceedingly sensitive time when it doesn't take much to stir things up. Fortunately, because we have gone through this with other couples a few thousand times a year for decades, we know exactly what you can do, and the kinds of things you must avoid, to make breaking up as smooth as possible.

1. Alternatives if you're not sure

If one of you decides it is definitely over, then it is definitely over for both. You can't make an unwilling person stay. But, if you are both open to the possibility of at least trying to save your relationship, there are steps you can take and people who can help you. If you signed a Couples Contract, you have already committed yourselves to making use of these resources in case of trouble in the relationship.

Counseling. Sometimes the intervention of a third party can help a great deal, especially when it is difficult for you to talk to each other about your problems. Consider getting help from a marriage or couples counselor, religious advisor, or other trained and certified professional. John Gottman's best-seller, *The Seven Principles for Making Marriage Work,* points out that building up the positive features of your relationship is even more important than resolving conflicts (chapter 1B(2)), and many couples counselors now work from this perspective.

Trial separation. A trial separation can provide a cooling-off period that helps to settle your emotions and clear your thinking. It might help you realize that being together is still better than being apart, and it gives you a comfortable situation from which to work on reconciliation. If you are concerned about your spouse mismanaging community funds or assets, a trial separation may not be a

---

[1] For couples who are not married, breaking up presents similar challenges. In this discussion, if you replace *divorce* with *breakup* and *spouse* with *partner,* it will work the same for you.

good idea unless you can make arrangements that will put that worry to rest. You also have to make practical arrangements for paying bills for both spouses and parenting if you have children. Legally, however, there is nothing you need to do—just go ahead and arrange your trial separation, and good luck.

Divorce counseling is also widely available and we highly recommend it, especially if you have children. In this case, the idea is not to get back together, but to separate decently.

2.   If you decide to separate—setting the tone

If you decide to separate, don't do one more thing or say one more word to your spouse until you've read the rest of this chapter. The way you announce the decision, or respond to it, will make a huge difference in the way things unwind.

The most common cause of conflict in separation and divorce is lack of mutuality in the decision—in other words, both spouses haven't accepted the idea that you're breaking up. Ideally, the decision would be arrived at together, but in most cases one spouse decides alone after taking time to think about it, get advice from friends or professionals, process emotions, and make plans.

Once the decision is made, it is presented to the other spouse as a done deal and the sooner the better. Opportunities to solve problems and possibly save the relationship have been lost. What's worse, a long, hard divorce is more likely because the first spouse is ready to break up right away while the other spouse is upset and still working through denial and resistance. This person hasn't had time to process the reality and will be in some kind of emotional upset, in no way ready to discuss details or work out accommodations.

This is not a good time to push along on the breakup, even though the first spouse is ready and highly motivated to do so. Moving along too quickly at this point is the root cause of a lot of trouble to follow.

Advice for the first to decide. You are in a unique and powerful position to affect the future tone of the divorce. By being abrupt and insensitive, you can almost guarantee a bitter, expensive divorce. If you want to encourage a sane resolution of divorce issues, be patient, be sensitive, but most of all, slow down. Give your spouse time to process the changes. Stay positive and as close to your spouse as possible. You can express caring and concern while being firm in your decision. Work with your spouse until you can both accept the fact that going your separate ways is inevitable, and you can both focus on moving forward.

3.   Can you stop a divorce?

Yes, and no. If you both agree you want to work on your relationship and try for a reconciliation, the two of you together can stop the divorce any time, right up to the day the judgment becomes final. But after a divorce petition is filed in court, one spouse cannot stop a divorce by contesting it. A court will not consider whether there are really "irreconcilable differences." If one spouse says there are irreconcilable differences and the other says there aren't, that's an irreconcilable difference. If you think you can work things out, try to persuade your spouse, not a lawyer or judge. Of course, you want a fair deal on the terms, but if you simply try to obstruct a divorce, you only guarantee that some attorneys will make a lot of money and you will end up hurting yourself and your children for no gain.

4.   The five causes of conflict[2]

To reduce conflict, you have to avoid or overcome the forces that create it. There are four or five in every case:

a.   Emotional upset and conflict. This is about high levels of anger, hurt, blame, and guilt—a very normal part of divorce. If one or both spouses is upset, you can't negotiate, have reasonable discussions or make sound decisions. Complex and volatile emotions become externalized—attached to things or to the children. When emotions are high, reason is at its lowest and will not be very effective *at that time.*

b.   Insecurity, fear, lack of confidence, unequal bargaining power. You can't negotiate if either spouse feels incompetent, afraid, or that the other spouse has some big advantage. Divorce is tremendously undermining; it tends to multiply any lack of self-confidence, and there are often real causes for insecurity: lack of skill and experience at dealing with business and negotiation, and lack of complete information and knowledge about the process and the marital affairs. It doesn't matter if insecurity is real or reasonable; it *is* real if it *feels* real.

c.   Ignorance and misinformation. Ignorance about the legal system and how it works can make you feel uncertain, insecure and incompetent. You feel as if you don't know what you are doing . . . and you are right! Misinformation is when the things you think you know are not correct. Misinformation comes from

---

[2] Sections 4 through 11 are summaries of material discussed at greater length in Nolo's award-winning book, *Divorce Solutions: How to Make Any Divorce Better.*

friends, television, movies, even from lawyers who are not family law specialists. It can distort your expectations about your rights and what's fair. It's hard to negotiate with someone who has mistaken ideas about what the rules are. Fortunately, both conditions can be easily fixed with *reliable* information.

d. The legal system and lawyers. The legal system is one of the most insidious contributors to conflict and expense in divorce cases. The legal system is by nature *adversarial*; it is based on the principle of conflict, one side struggling against the other trying to win. If you retain an attorney to "take" your case, you will probably be dragged into the legal system and this is not what you want in a divorce. Few lawyers can help you talk to your spouse rationally or overcome emotional upset; most are more likely to reinforce it. Attorneys are paid by the hour, so they have no financial incentive to encourage an amicable resolution. (An exception to dysfunctional legal service can be found in the offices of those few attorneys who have abandoned litigation almost entirely in favor of practicing "collaborative law," described in section 8 below).

In all but the most conflicted divorces, you want to avoid the legal system as much as possible and—with the help of your Couples Contract and other Nolo books—you can. Unless you are facing immediate threat of harm to yourself, your children or your property, it would be better not to *retain* an attorney, though it is usually a good idea to get advice from one. Before you seek legal assistance, it would help to read Nolo's *Divorce Solutions: How to Make Any Divorce Better.*

e. Real disagreement. These are the real issues that you want to deal with rationally and negotiate with your spouse. Real disagreement is based on the fact that the spouses now have different needs and interests. After dealing with the first four obstacles, these real issues may turn out to be minor, but even if they are serious, at least they can be negotiated rationally.

The solutions are in your hands. Apart from the legal system—which you can avoid—all obstacles to your agreement are personal, between you and your spouse and between you and yourself. The solutions are entirely in your own hands and the legal system has little to offer compared with the potential for harm, especially compared with all the things you can do for yourself outside the legal system.

Take care. Pay special attention to emotional upset and especially insecurity and fear. These are the forces that drive people into a lawyer's office. You want to avoid doing anything that might increase the upset and fear of either spouse.

- The upset person is saying, "I can't stand this, I won't take it anymore! I'm going to get a lawyer!"

- The insecure person is saying, "I can't understand all this, I can't deal with it, I can't deal with my spouse. I want to be safe. I need someone to help me. I'm going to get a lawyer."

This is how cases get dragged into unnecessary legal conflict.

5. How to reduce conflict

Once breaking up becomes a reality, there are very practical and effective things you can do to deal with the forces that create conflict. They might not all be of use in every case, so just use what applies to you.

a. Make some "new life" resolutions. Start thinking of yourself as a whole and separate person. You may feel wounded, but you are healing and becoming whole and complete. Keep that picture in mind. Pain and confusion are part of healing. Let go of old attachments, old dreams, old patterns that don't work; this is your chance to build new ones. Decide you will not be a victim of your spouse or the system or yourself. You will not try to change or control your spouse—that's all over now, it doesn't work, it's contrary to the meaning of divorce. Concentrate on yourself, especially on your own actions. You can do something about what your spouse does by changing what you do. Take responsibility for yourself: if anyone hurts or upsets you, try to understand how you let them do that. Try to become quiet and calm. Keep your life as simple as possible.

b. Insulate and protect your children. Involving children will harm them and upset the parents. Keep children away from the divorce. Tell them the truth in simple terms they can understand, but otherwise don't discuss the divorce in front of them or pass messages through them. Don't let them hear your arguments or hear you criticize their other parent. Let them know you both love them and will always be their mother and father, no matter what happens between you. Help them understand that loving their other parent is not a betrayal of you; they shouldn't have to choose sides. Help them establish a new pattern of stability so they feel safe, and help them have as much contact as possible with both parents.

c. Get safe, stable and secure, just for a while. Your first and most important job is to do *whatever* you have to do to arrange short-term safety, stability, and security for yourself, the children, and your spouse—in that order. This doesn't mean forever, just for a month or a few months at a time. Don't be concerned yet about the long term or the final outcome, and we're talking about minimum conditions here, not your old standard of living. Don't even try to do anything else until minimum conditions are met. You can't negotiate if you don't know where you will live or how you will eat, or if you are afraid for your safety or if you think your house is about to be foreclosed or your car repossessed. You can't negotiate if your spouse is not in a safe and stable situation, too. As much as possible, help each other become stable, otherwise the fear and upset level will go up, so that even if you stay out of court because of your agreement to arbitrate, the process will get more complicated and expensive. You might even get dragged into court at an early stage, despite your agreement to use mediation and arbitration (ADR), if one of you, out of desperation, creates an emergency situation before ADR gets started. These legal procedures are tremendously upsetting and *very* expensive, on the order of tens of thousands of dollars for each side. To avoid this kind of outcome, you have to help each other even if you don't feel like it.

d. Agree on temporary arrangements. It takes a long time for things to settle down and for the spouses to work out a final agreement. Meanwhile, you have to arrange for the support of two households on the same old income, the parenting of minor children, making payments on mortgages and debts, and so on. Ideally, arrangements for such things will be set out in writing.

If you can work out your own temporary arrangements during separation, neither spouse will need an attorney to get temporary court orders. Start by agreeing that you want a fair result and will both act fairly. Agree to communicate before doing anything that will affect the other spouse or the estate or the children. Agree on a mediator and meet with him or her as soon as possible. The goal here is to avoid surprises and upset. Among other things, that includes closing joint accounts or starting legal actions.

e. Slow down, take some time. If you can make your situation safe and stable for a while, you don't have to be in a hurry. Think of divorce as an illness or an accident; it really is a kind of injury, and it takes time to heal. You have to go slow and easy. Some very important work goes on during this slowdown. You work on reducing emotional upset—this takes time. You work on mutual acceptance—this takes time. You work to help both spouses become confident, stable, secure. Use this time to get reliable information and advice; find out what the rules are; line up the mediation/arbitration services you agreed to use in your Couples Contract.

f. Get information and advice. First, organize your facts, records and documents. You'll want lists of assets, deeds, statements, account numbers, income and expense information, tax returns and wage stubs. Get information from your records, from your accountant, from recent tax returns, and from your spouse. Spouses should have a full and open exchange of information; it helps to build trust and confidence—and it's the law, so you might as well just go ahead and do it. If information is not exchanged freely outside of the legal system, you will probably end up in court with attorneys doing very expensive discovery work.

Learn the rules as they apply to your case. Read Nolo's best-seller, *Divorce Solutions: How to Make Any Divorce Better* and in California or Texas, get *How to Do Your Own Divorce*. Make sure your spouse has a copy of these books, then maybe you can discuss some of the issues and ideas in them.

Be *very* careful where you get advice. Friends and relatives will want to help, but while emotional support is welcome, when they offer legal and financial advice, *don't take it*—the price is too high if they're wrong. They mean well, but probably don't know what they're talking about. Don't take advice from paralegals or forms typing services; they're not trained for it.

g. Focus on needs and interests; don't take positions yet or get attached to a particular outcome. A position is a stand on a final outcome: "I want the house sold and the children every weekend." In the beginning, there's too much upset and too little information to decide what you want for an outcome and, besides, positions are a setup for an argument: the other side either agrees or disagrees. It's better to think and talk in terms of needs and interests. These are more basic concerns: "I want what's fair and what the rules say is mine; I need to be secure and have enough to live on; I want to know what I can count on for living expenses; I want maximum contact with my children; I need to get out of debt, especially on the credit cards; I want an end to argument and upset." Put this way, these are goals that you and your spouse can discuss together. If you get attached too early to a particular outcome, you'll close off other available options.

h. Stick with short-term solutions. Concentrate on short-term solutions to immediate problems, like keeping two separate households afloat for a few months; keeping mortgages paid and cars from being repossessed; keeping children protected, secure, stable, in contact with both parents. These are things you can possibly work on together.

i. Minimize legal activity. Avoid legal activity unless it is absolutely necessary—zero is best, or the minimum required to protect yourself or just get your case started, but do nothing else until you've arranged mediation and arbitration. Getting legal advice is a good idea, but it is best to avoid retaining an attorney and you don't want to give your spouse any reason to retain one either.

j. Get help if you need it. Consider counseling or therapy for yourself or children. For help with talking to your spouse, consider couples counseling or see a mediator. These low-conflict professionals can help with emotional issues, defusing upset or, in the case of the mediator, making temporary arrangements.

6. What divorce is really about

To get a divorce (dissolution of marriage), you have to settle these issues:
- How to divide whatever property and debts have accumulated during the marriage; and
- If there will be spousal support; and, if so, how much and for how long.

If you have minor children, you must also decide:
- How parents will share the care and duties of raising the children; and
- How much will be paid for child support.

As far as the law is concerned, this is what a divorce is about—property, children and support. If you can't settle these issues between you, a third person—a judge or arbitrator—who doesn't know you or your family, will take as little time as possible to make the decisions for you. Whether you do it yourself or an attorney does it, you still have to gather your own facts and make your own decisions as to what you want to do, so you might as well do most or all of it yourself.

It is far better if couples who can't agree on some issues would agree to settle the matter through negotiation or mediation rather than arbitration or court. Even then, arbitration is the better choice. Family resources should be split between the partners to a marriage rather than the partners in a law firm.

7. Should you do your own divorce?

Yes! You *can* do your own divorce. Since Nolo's *How to Do Your Own Divorce in California* (or *Texas*) was first published, millions of people just like you have done their divorces without retaining lawyers, so you can almost certainly do it too. *How to Do Your Own Divorce* tells you what the rules are and how things are normally done. It helps you make your decisions, then shows you how to get your case through the courts. Some other states also have books on this subject.

You *should* do your own divorce. The legal process—and the way attorneys work in it—tends to cause trouble, raise the level of conflict and greatly increase your expense. Whether using mediation/arbitration, or going straight to court, no one should *retain* an attorney in a divorce case unless it is absolutely necessary. This does not mean you can't get advice, information or help from an attorney, just that you should not retain one to *take* your case and try to do it all for you.

There are a few cases where you should *not* do your own divorce. You should retain an attorney if there is an immediate threat of harm to you or your children, or if your spouse is trying to transfer valuable assets. You may need help if your spouse is on *active* military duty and will not sign a waiver.

8. Who can help?

Nolo books. *Divorce Solutions: How to Make Any Divorce Better* gives you practical advice about getting through the emotional, practical and financial obstacles that you face. It's about how to deal with your spouse, how to negotiate, and how to keep your divorce sane. This best-seller may save you thousands of dollars and lots of pain. Get a copy and one for your spouse, too. Shared information works better. It will be the best money you ever spent.

Friends, relatives and "common knowledge" are the worst and most expensive sources of advice. Use them for moral support, but when they give you advice, say "thank you," but check with a reliable source before taking it. If you didn't get it from a *current* Nolo book or a family law specialist attorney in your state, *don't trust it!* Just because you like or trust someone doesn't make them right. Bad advice can cost you dearly—perhaps for the rest of your life.

Typing services. Many states have a sub-profession of non-attorneys who help you fill out and file forms and get a divorce, sometimes called "independent paralegals" or "Legal Document Assistants." In theory, these people act as a typing service for people doing their own divorces. You tell them exactly what you want and they type up the forms, help you file them with the court, and handle the secretarial work. Many attorneys are convinced they do far more, and without training or license. Their rates are usually very affordable, especially compared to hiring an attorney. We introduced this innovation in legal service in California in 1972 and it has since changed the face of the legal map in many states.

It is very important for you to understand the limitations of typing services. Some are trained, but no training or other qualifications are necessary—anyone can do it. You *can't* get reliable legal advice from these people, nor can they safely prepare your marital settlement agreement (MSA) unless you have a *very* simple case and not enough property to be concerned about.

There are many good services out there, but be careful who you hire, just as when hiring a lawyer or a mechanic. Ask how long they have been in business and be sure to check references. If you know *exactly* what you want and have no legal questions, no problems, and have only the simplest MSA, then using an experienced and reliable service is a very good way to get your paperwork done.

Lawyers. Hourly rates in urban areas can run over $400, but $150–250 per hour is common. When you retain an attorney to take your case, you will be asked to pay a retainer fee at the beginning. About $2,000–5,000 is typical, but the amount doesn't matter because the final bill will almost certainly be much higher. Few attorneys will give you a fixed fee for the whole job. You are doing *very* well if you end up spending less than $2,500 *per spouse* on the *simplest* case; the average in urban areas when both spouses are represented is over $18,000 *per spouse!*

Because of the way the system works and the way lawyers work, an attorney who takes charge of your case will almost certainly create unnecessary conflict and expense, so do not *retain* an attorney unless there's no other choice. Short of retaining an attorney, it is often a good idea to get information and advice from an attorney who won't use the consultation to convince you that your case is so complicated and difficult that you need him/her to take your case and represent you. Your best advice will come from attorneys who primarily do mediation and little or no litigation, as they are more oriented toward problem-solving. Before going to an attorney for any purpose, you should read Nolo's *Divorce Solutions,* organize your facts and documents, and write down everything you want to ask.

Collaborative lawyers. Recently, collaborative law has emerged as another option to mediation or litigation. Increasingly popular, in this approach the spouses each have an attorney on their side, but the attorneys pledge in writing not go to court or even threaten to go to court. Instead, they will use negotiation and mediation to solve problems and reach a settlement. If there's no settlement, the spouses will have to get different attorneys to take the case into litigation. Ideally, the collaborative team will include some other professionals, such as a divorce coach, family counselor, child specialist, accountant, or financial planner. Collaborative divorce has a good track record and, even with all the professional services you get, it will still cost less than a court battle.

9. Children of divorce

Fighting over your kids—custody, visitation, parenting—is the worst possible thing that can happen to you or your kids. It's always ugly. Studies show that harm to children is more closely related to conflict *after* the divorce. Everyone has conflict before and during a divorce, but if you want to help your children, get finished with the conflict and resolve it as soon as possible, at least within yourself.

Children need a relationship with both parents because of bonding that can't be replaced by a surrogate or stepparent. To protect your children, you have to insulate them from your own conflict with their other parent. The divorce is not their problem; it's yours. Being a bad wife or husband does not necessarily make your spouse a bad parent. So, don't hold the children hostage—they are not pawns or bartering pieces in your game. In the area of custody and visitation, don't bargain with your spouse on any basis other than what will give your children the most stability and the best contact with both parents.

The worst thing for the child is feeling responsible for the breakup and feeling that loving one parent is a betrayal of the other. These feelings cause children intense stress and insecurity. To protect your child from almost unbearable pain, don't say anything bad about the other parent in front of the child; don't undermine or interfere in any way with the child's relationship with or love for the other parent; don't put the child in a position of having to take sides. Do encourage every possible kind of constructive relationship your child can have with your ex-mate. Let the children know that you are happy when they have a good, loving time with their other parent.

Kids can really get on your nerves at times and single parenting is enough to overwhelm any normal person. You are not Superman or Wonder Woman and kids are not designed to be raised by one lone person. You need help and support and some time off from the kids. Get help from family, friends and the many parent support groups and family service agencies in your state. Get referrals to groups in your area through temples, churches, the court, or social service agencies.

10. Ten ways to divide property without a fight

If dividing your property is a problem, here are ten ways it can be done without a fight. Even if you agreed to use mediation/arbitration in your Couples Contract, the more things you can work out on your own, the better. Just talk it over and agree to use a method that you can both accept. This list was originally developed by Judge Robert K. Garth of Riverside, California.

1. Barter. Each party takes certain items of property in exchange for other items. For instance, the car and furniture in exchange for the truck and tools. Let's make a deal!

2. Choose items alternately. The spouses take turns selecting items from a list of all the marital property, without regard for the value of items selected.

3. One divides, the other chooses. One spouse divides all the marital property into two parts and the other spouse gets the choice of parts.

4. One values, the other chooses. One spouse places a value on each item of marital property and the other spouse gets the choice of items up to an agreed share of the total value.

5. Appraisal and alternate selection. A third person (such as an appraiser) agreed upon by the parties places a value on contested items of marital property and the parties choose alternately until one spouse has chosen items worth his or her share of the marital property.

6. Sale. Some or all of the marital property is sold and the proceeds divided.

7. Secret bids. The spouses place secret bids on each item of marital property and the one who bids highest for an item gets it. Where one receives items that exceed his or her share of the total value, there will be an equalization payment to the other spouse.

8. Private auction. The spouses openly bid against each other on each item of marital property. If one spouse gets more than their share, an equalization payment can be made.

9. Arbitration. The spouses select an arbitrator who will decide the matter of valuation and division after hearing from both spouses and considering all evidence.

10. Mediation. The spouses select a mediator who works to help them reach an agreement on matters of valuation and division.

11. How to negotiate with your spouse

a. Get information and advice. Use the Nolo Press books, *How to Do Your Own Divorce* (California or Texas) and *Divorce Solutions: How to Make Any Divorce Better*. Give your spouse these books. In California, call Divorce Helpline and talk to one of our consulting attorneys who will help you develop options. The toll-free number is (800) 359-7004 in California. For other states, check the reference desk of your public library or see a family law attorney for information and suggestions for options you can pursue.

b. Be prepared. Get the facts about your assets, debts, income and expenses and help your spouse get the facts, too. Make sure you understand the rules that apply to your facts.

c. Be businesslike

- Keep business and personal matters separate.
- Meet in a neutral place where you can be free of interruptions.
- Make appointments to meet; be on time; make an agenda ahead of time.
- Be polite and insist on reasonable manners in return. If things become unbusinesslike, ask to set another date to continue the discussion.

d. Problem solving. Approach your negotiations as problem-solving sessions—something you work on together.

e. Balance the negotiating power

- If you feel insecure, become informed, be well prepared, use an agenda, get advice from a reliable source. Don't feel pressured into responses or arguments; state your ideas, listen to your spouse, think it over until the next meeting. Get advice if you feel it might help. Don't continue if you aren't calm or if the meeting doesn't stay businesslike. Consider using professional mediation.

- If you are the more confident spouse, help build your spouse's confidence so he or she can negotiate confidently. Share all information openly. Be a super listener. Restate what your spouse says to show you've heard it. Don't respond immediately, but take time to think about what you've heard. Tone yourself back: state your points clearly but don't try to persuade or repeat yourself. Listen, listen, listen.

f. State issues in a constructive way. Instead of, "I want the house," say, "The house is very important to me because . . . ." The second statement encourages discussion and negotiation.

g. Build agreement. Start with the facts and don't go forward until you both agree to the facts about your property, income, expenses, and debts. Write down the facts you agree on and those you don't. Do research and exchange documents to resolve differences. Compromise. Make a list of issues you agree on. Try to refine the issues you do not agree on and make them more clear and precise.

h. Be patient and persistent. It takes time for people to accept new ideas and adjust their thinking. Don't be in a hurry; don't be surprised at upsets and reversals. Things will almost always resolve themselves later.

i. Get help. If you think your case is blowing up, don't give up. This is exactly the time to consult a family law attorney-mediator in your state (chapter 3B).

j. Mediation. When you and your spouse have come to an impasse on an issue or a group of issues and need a guide to help you find your way, a good mediator may be the right prescription. When you look for a professional mediator, choose one who is also a family law attorney. Non-attorney mediators do not feel comfortable with the legal issues in a divorce. The best way to find a mediator is by recommendation from someone you trust.

Mediation is not marriage counseling and is not used to get back together with your spouse, although if this is something you might be open to, you should tell your mediator and ask his or her attitude about working with couples in that situation. You should look at mediation as a positive step taken to resolve your disagreements that will help direct you and your spouse toward a fair settlement.

12. Last words

Hard times or difficult problems do not necessarily mean your relationship is over. Talk over the process you went through when deciding to make a life together and crafting your Couples Contract, if you made one. Recall your promises and intentions back then and what you agreed to. Remember your dream for a lasting relationship together.

Statistics tell us that two-thirds of all couples who stayed together through a very unhappy marriage reported five years later that their marriages were happy. Even if you've discussed the possibility of separation or divorce, your relationship may not be over. Consider your options and get help from your community and professionals. Consider resources like Retrouvaille (www.retrouvaille.org), that specialize in helping couples deal with severely troubled relationships.

You began your relationship making plans and choices together. Even though not all relationships last a lifetime, many do, so yours can. The choices are still yours. Take every opportunity to realize your commitments and hopes. No matter what, we wish you the very best!

APPENDIX

B

Nolo Supplementary Family Arbitration Rules

Arbitration rules have been published by many organizations that provide arbitration services, such as the American Arbitration Association, Peacemaker Ministries, and the Beth Din of America. Arbitration rules that apply in cases in which the parties have not specified rules have been enacted by law in many states.

These rules have in general been adopted with business disputes in mind and therefore do not provide for the kinds of temporary, preliminary or interim measures that are often necessary in family disputes or circumstances of marital separation. They also do not provide for the kinds of post-judgment relief and modifications that are sometimes necessary in family disputes.

To fill this gap, we created the Nolo Supplementary Family Arbitration Rules, which are intended to supplement any set of arbitration rules a couple might adopt, in order to deal with situations not anticipated by most sets of arbitration rules currently published by recognized organizations.

Exhibit A
Nolo Supplementary Family Arbitration Rules
Nolo Press Occidental • www.nolocouples.com

1. Scope and application

Any dispute subject to arbitration pursuant to a premarital, postmarital, living together, marital settlement agreement, couples contract or relationship agreement that refers to these rules will be governed by the arbitration rules named in the agreement or otherwise selected by the parties, except that interim and post-judgment matters shall be governed by the following supplementary rules:

2. Interim relief and interim measures

(a) In the case of an arbitration where arbitrators have not yet been appointed, or where the arbitrators are unavailable, a party may seek interim remedies directly from a court as provided in subsection (c) of this section. Enforcement shall be granted as provided by the laws of the state in which the interim relief is sought.

(b) In all other cases, including cases of modification of interim relief obtained directly from a court prior to commencement of the arbitration or under subsection (a) of this section, a party shall seek interim measures as described in subsection (d) of this section from the arbitrators. A party has no right to seek interim relief from a court, except that a party to an arbitration governed by this Article may request from the court enforcement of the arbitrators' order granting interim measures and review or modification of any interim measures governing child support or child custody.

(c) In connection with an agreement to arbitrate or a pending arbitration, the court may grant under subsection (a) of this section any temporary or *pendente lite* orders a court is permitted by state law to make during the pendency of a family law proceeding, including but not limited to:

(1) A temporary restraining order or preliminary injunction;

(2) An order for temporary child custody and visitation while the arbitration is pending or until a judgment may be entered on the arbitration award;

(3) An order for temporary support of any party or child of the parties while the arbitration is pending or until a judgment may be entered on the arbitration award;

(4) An order for temporary possession and control of real or personal property of the parties;

(5) An order for the immediate sale of any asset of the parties;

(6) An order for payment of debts and obligations of the parties;

(7) Any other order necessary to ensure preservation or availability of assets or documents, the destruction or absence of which would likely prejudice the conduct or effectiveness of the arbitration.

(d) The arbitrators may, at a party's request, order any party to take any interim measures of protection that the arbitrators consider necessary in respect to the subject matter of the dispute, including interim measures analogous to interim relief specified in subsection (c) of this section. The arbitrators may require any party to provide appropriate security in connection with interim measures.

(e) In considering a request for interim relief or enforcement of interim relief, any finding of fact of the arbitrators in the proceeding shall be binding on the court, including any finding regarding the probable validity of the claim that is the subject of the interim relief sought or granted, except that the court may review any findings of fact or modify any interim measures governing child support or child custody.

(f) Where the arbitrators have not ruled on an objection to their jurisdiction, the findings of the arbitrators shall not be binding on the court until the court has made an independent finding as to the arbitrators' jurisdiction. If the court rules that the arbitrators do not have jurisdiction, the application for interim relief shall be denied.

(g) Availability of interim relief or interim measures under this section may be limited by the parties' prior written agreement, except for relief whose purpose is to provide immediate, emergency relief or protection, or relief directly related to the welfare of a child.

(h) Arbitrators who have cause to suspect that any child is abused or neglected shall report the case of that child to the appropriate child protection authorities of the county where the child resides or, if the child resides out-of-state, of the county where the arbitration is conducted.

(i) A party seeking interim measures, or any other proceeding before the arbitrators, shall proceed in accordance with the agreement to arbitrate. If the agreement to arbitrate does not provide for a method of seeking interim measures, or for other proceedings before the arbitrators, the party shall request interim measures or a hearing by notifying the arbitrators and all other parties of the request. The arbitrators shall notify the parties of the date, time, and place of the hearing.

3. Post-judgment modification and other relief

(a) In the case of any dispute which may arise after the conclusion of the original arbitration proceedings or after a court has entered a judgment between the parties, requests for modification or set-aside of any matter shall be subject to arbitration to the extent and in the same manner and to the same extent as the arbitration of a prejudgment dispute between the parties.

(b) Where arbitrators have not yet been appointed, or where the arbitrators are unavailable, a party may seek post-judgment modification relief directly from a court as provided in subsection (d) of this section. Enforcement shall be granted as provided by the law applicable to the type of post-judgment relief sought. A party may not seek directly from a court a set-aside of a judgment based on an arbitration award. The arbitrators shall have exclusive jurisdiction over such matters, except that a party to an arbitration governed by this Article may request from the court enforcement of the arbitrator's order granting such post-judgment measures.

(c) In all other cases a party shall seek post-judgment measures as described in subsection (e) of this section from the arbitrators. A party has no right to seek post-judgment relief from a court, except that a party to an arbitration governed by this Article may request from the court enforcement of the arbitrators' order granting post-judgment measures and review or modification of any post-judgment measures governing child support or child custody.

(d) In connection with an agreement to arbitrate or a pending arbitration, the court may grant under subsection (b) of this section any orders a court is permitted by state law to make upon a showing of changed circumstances after entry of judgment in a family law proceeding, including but not limited to:

(1) A restraining order or injunction;

(2) An order for modification of child custody and visitation;

(3) An order for modification of support of any party or child of the parties after judgment;

(4) Any other order necessary to ensure preservation or availability of assets or documents, the destruction or absence of which would likely prejudice the conduct or effectiveness of the arbitration.

(e) The arbitrators may, at a party's request, make any post-judgment orders the arbitrators consider necessary in respect to the subject matter of the dispute, including post-judgment measures analogous to post-judgment relief specified in subsection (d) of this section. The arbitrators may require any party to provide appropriate security in connection with post-judgment measures.

(f) In considering a request for post-judgment relief or enforcement of post-judgment relief, any finding of fact of the arbitrators in the proceeding shall be binding on the court, including any finding regarding the probable validity of the claim that is the subject of the post-judgment relief sought or granted, except that the court may review any findings of fact or modify any post-judgment measures governing child support or child custody.

(g) Where the arbitrators have not ruled on an objection to their jurisdiction, the findings of the arbitrators shall not be binding on the court until the court has made an independent finding as to the arbitrators' jurisdiction. If the court rules that the arbitrators do not have jurisdiction, the application for post-judgment relief shall be denied.

(h) Availability of post-judgment relief or post-judgment measures under this section may be limited by the parties' prior written agreement, except for relief whose purpose is to provide immediate, emergency relief or protection, or relief directly related to the welfare of a child.

(i) Arbitrators who have cause to suspect that any child is abused or neglected shall report the case of that child to the appropriate child protection authorities of the county where the child resides or, if the child resides out-of-state, of the county where the arbitration is conducted.

(j) A party seeking post-judgment measures, or any other proceeding before the arbitrators, shall proceed in accordance with the agreement to arbitrate. If the agreement to arbitrate does not provide for a method of seeking post-judgment measures, or for other proceedings before the arbitrators, the party shall request post-judgment measures or a hearing by notifying the arbitrators and all other parties of the request. The arbitrators shall notify the parties of the date, time, and place of the hearing.

C

Relationship resources*

Relationship

A Couple's Guide to Communication, Gottman, Notarius, Gonso, and Markman

All You Need Is Love & Other Lies About Marriage, John W. Jacobs, MD

The Couple Communication Program: www.couplecommunication.com

Couples Helpline: www.coupleshelpline.com

The Couple's Survival Workbook, David Olsen and Douglas Stephens

The Divorce Remedy: The Proven 7-Step Program for Saving Your Marriage, Michele Weiner Davis

Fighting for Your Marriage, Howard J. Markman, Scott M. Stanley, Susan L. Blumberg

The Five Love Languages, Gary Chapman

Getting the Love You Want, Harville Hendrix

The Gottman Institute: www.gottman.com

The Heart's Wisdom:
A Practical Guide to Growing Through Love, Barry and Joyce Vissel

How To Get The Most From Couples Therapy, Peter Pearson (on CD, Resources folder)

Love Knots: How to Untangle Those Everyday Frustrations, Lori H. Gordon

Marriage Encounter: www.marriage-encounter.org

Passage to Intimacy, Gordon and Frandsen

Reconcilable Differences, Andrew Christensen and Neil S. Jacobson

The Relationship Cure, John Gottman

Retrouvaille: A Lifeline for Married Couples: www.retrouvaille.org

Risk To Be Healed, Barry and Joyce Vissell

The Seven Principles for a Making Marriage Work: A Practical Guide, John Gottman and Nan Silver

The Shared Heart Foundation: www.sharedheart.org

Smart Marriages: www.smartmarriages.com

Tell Me No Lies: How to Face the Truth and Build a Loving Marriage, Bader and Pearson

Why Am I Afraid to Tell You Who I Am? John Powell

Why Marriages Succeed or Fail… and How You Can Make Yours Last, John Gottman

You Just Don't Understand, Deborah Tannen

---

*Recommended to their own clients (and now to you) by practicing professionals

Financial and estate planning

Aging With Dignity—5 Wishes:
www.AgingWithDignity.org

The Couple's Guide to Love & Money,
Jonathan Rich, PhD

Debtors Anonymous:
www.debtorsanonymous.org

*Facing Financial Dysfunction: Why Smart
People Do Stupid Things with Money,*
Bert Whitehead, MBA, JD

*How To Get Out of Debt, Stay Out of Debt,
and Live Prosperously,* Jerrold Mundis

Just Give Me the Answers, Sheryl Garrett
et. al.

Legal Affairs, Frederick Hertz

The Millionaire Next Door, Stanley and
Danke

The Seven Stages of Money Maturity,
George Kinder

Smart Couples Finish Rich, David Bach

The Soul of Money, Lynn Twist

Unmarried America:
www.UnmarriedAmerica.org

Unmarried to Each Other, Dorian Solot and
Marshall Miller

The Wealthy Spirit, Chellie Campbell

Your Money or Your LIfe, Joe Dominguez
and Vicki Robin

Faith

Beth Din of America: www.bethdin.org

*Celebrating Our Differences:
Living Two Faiths in One Marriage,*
Rosenbaum & Rosenbaum

The Dovetail Institute:
www.dovetailinstitute.org

Marriage Encounter:
www.marriage-encounter.org

Peacemaker Ministries & Christian Conciliation: www.HisPeace.org

Retrouvaille: A Lifeline for Married Couples:
www.retrouvaille.org

APPENDIX

D

How to use the CD and the files

How to open the CD

- **Windows.** If the CD does not open automatically, navigate to your CD drive to view files listed on it. Click on "Start CD" to start the interface or simply browse the folders manually.
- **Mac.** When the CD mounts on your desktop, double-click to open it and view the folders and files on it. If your Mac has a Windows environment, open the CD there to take advantage of the handy CD interface.

Finding files

- All clauses and documents are organized according to the chapter in which they are mentioned, except the Basic Contract Kit and the Nolo Arbitration Rules, which are located in their own folders.
- Additional files of interest are found in the folder Resources & Extras.
- Ignore the folder "Auto_G." It contains files that operate the CD interface on Windows computers.

Using the files

- Copy files you want to work with to a convenient folder on your computer.
- All contract clauses and documents are in RTF format, which can be opened from any word processor. Edit the basic Couples Contract and any variations you add to create your own agreement.
- **To open a file.** If you double-click the file, it might bring up your word processor automatically. If not, open your word processor and under the File menu, select Open and navigate to the file you want to work with, then either double-click the file you want or select the file and click the Open or OK button.
- Edit the files as described in section 3C.

- **PDF files.** The Disclosure Worksheet, Checklist, Legal Briefs, Nolo Rules and some articles are in PDF format, which you can view and print with the free program Adobe Reader. Version 5.1 or later is required, but version 6.0 or later is recommended. If you don't have the latest Adobe Reader on your computer, go to www.adobe.com and get the latest version for your particular operating system.
- **The Worksheet.** The free Reader program does not allow you to save data you have entered, so start by printing a blank form and filling it out by hand. When it looks exactly right, you can fill it out on your computer and print it.
- If you want to save data you enter in the Disclosure Worksheet:

  — **Widows users.** You can download Cute PDF Form Filler for $30 from www.cutepdf.com.

  — **Mac users.** Mac OS X lets you save your completed PDF form. Simply select File > Print, then click on the PDF button and select Save as PDF. For OS 9 or earlier, there are shareware applications that allow you to do the same thing. We like PrintToPDF ($20), which you can get from their Web site at www.jwwalker.com/pages/pdf.html.

  If you can borrow a Windows computer or find a Mac with Virtual PC, you can use Cute PDF Form Filler, described above.

  If you have OS X, you can go online and purchase one of the utilities lilsted below. Be sure to get free trial versions and test them before you decide which one you want to use.

  PDFpen ($49.95) www.smileonmymac.com/PDFpen/
  pdf-FormServer ($44.33)
  http://shop.pdf-office.com/
  product_info.php?products_id=29&language=en
  FormMate ($29.95) www.whitewolf.com/FM/FMIntro.htm

Be safe!

- Save your work frequently.
- Make a backup copy of your file by saving it onto a floppy disk or CD and keep the backup copy somewhere safe.

Index

E

F

G

H

I

income and assets, 65, 129, 142–45
inheritance issues, 152–53
insurance, health, 150–51
interfaith couples, agreements for, 123–24
Islamic marriage contract (*Aqd*), 102

J

Jewish Law (*Halakha*), 117
joint accounts for unmarried couples, 147–48
joint tenants, 64–65

K

Kelley Bluebook, 98
Ketubah, 102
"Kosher Coupling" column (Boteach), 103

L

last words, 193
laws. *See* legal relationships; unmarried couples, laws for
laws for unmarried couples. *See* unmarried couples, laws for
A Legal Guide for Lesbian & Gay Couples (Nolo), 154
legality of Contract, 48
legal relationships
    changeability of rules and, 62–63
    couples law in your state and, 64–68
    as defined by rules of law, 60
    events that bring rules into play, 61–62
    moving to another state, 19, 63–64, 154, 176
legal system, 183
libraries, 68
lifestyle agreements, 46–47, 123
Living Together (Nolo), 132, 154
living-together relationships. *See* unmarried couples
loss of consortium, 153

M

Make Your Own Living Trust (Nolo), 153
marital agreements, 159–60
marital estate, defined, 75
marital finances, defining, 76–77
Marriage Covenant (model), 113–14
Marriage Encounter, 19
marriages
    after retirement, 86–87, 89
    common-law, 67
    covenant, 112–17
    laws affecting, 66–67
    same-sex, 63, 73n
    See also commitments; legal relationships
Marvin palimony case, 146, 147
mediation
    arbitration and, 20–21, 185
    Couples Contract and, 38–39
    divorce and, 193
    faith-based agreements and, 103–04
    as relationship safety net, 19–21
medical concerns, 68
medical emergencies, 149–50
Modification of Relationship Agreement, 174–78
moving to another state, 19, 63–64, 154, 176

N

name changes, 149
"next of kin," 150
Nolo Supplementary Arbitration Rules (on CD), 136, 195–98
notarization of signatures, 51, 160, 166, 169, 174

O

oral agreements, 146
out-of-state property, 79
ownership
    forms of, 64–65
    terms of, 75

P

"palimony," 146

Parkinson, Father Joe, 103

partnership agreement, unmarried couples and, 131

partnerships, domestic, 48

paternity, 148

Peacemaker Ministries and Institute for Christian Conciliation, 105, 110–16

portability of contract, 178

premarital agreements, 13, 103, 159

property

    community, 64, 65n, 116

    division of, 190–91

    faith-based agreements and, 110

    out-of-state, 79

    separate, 57, 65, 75–76, 82–85

    transfers of, 172

    transmutation of, 65

    unmarried couples and, 147

    valuations of, 98

R

Rabbi Boteach, 103, 118

religious contracts, 102–03

resolutions for new life, 184

resources, relationship, 18–19, 67–70, 191–92, 199–200

reviews of Contract, periodic, 173

S

safety nets, relationship, 19–20

same-sex marriages, 63, 73n

Schedules 1 and 2, 44–45, 96–97, 99, 136

separate property, 57, 65, 75–76, 82–85

separation, trial, 180–81

Seven Principles for Making Marriage Work (Gottman), 17–18, 180

severability, 40–42

signatures, 44–45

    See also notarization of signatures

Signing Ceremony Script, 166–68

simplified financial disclosure, 96–97

Social Security, 151

spousal and child support, 80, 130, 142

spouses, surviving, 66

state laws, 19, 64–68

statement, disclosure, 96

storage of documents, 172

support, duty of, 147

support for unmarried partner, 142

supporting documents, 155–61

    Explanation of Agreement template, 156–58

    Waiver of Right to Independent Counsel and Acknowledgment of Receipt of Explanation, 159–61

T

tailoring, financial. *See* financial tailoring

taxes

    gift, 153n

    transfers of property and, 172

    unmarried couples and, 132, 135, 142, 148, 153

template for Couples Contract. *See* Couples Contracts, template for

tenants in common, 64–65

terminology of ownership, 64–65, 75

traditional contracts vs. Couples Contracts, 12–14

transfers of property, 172

transmutation of property, 65

Trans Union, 149

trial separation, 180–81

U

unmarried couples, 125–54

    advantages of written agreement, 67, 125–28

    breaking up, 180n

    changes to basic agreement by, 134–35

    commitment of, 132–34

    financial clarity and, 129–32

    income, defining, 129

    instructions for, 48, 73

BONUS CD
All clauses and Xtras

See Appendix D above for complete CD instructions

Windows

If the interface doesn't start automatically, open your CD drive in Explorer or from My Computer, then double click on the file "Start CD."

Mac

Double click on the CD icon on your desktop then browse through the folders. **Note:** If you have Virtual PC™ on your Mac, you can open a graphical CD interface by clicking on "Start CD."